The Four Tops

Iain McCartney

NEW HAVEN PUBLISHING LTD

Published 2024
First Edition
www.newhavenpublishingltd.com
newhavenpublishing@gmail.com

All Rights Reserved

The rights of Iain McCartney, as the author of this work, have been asserted in accordance with the Copyrights, Designs and Patents Act 1988.

No part of this book may be re-printed or reproduced or utilized in any form or by any electronic, mechanical or other means, now unknown or hereafter invented, including photocopying, and recording, or in any information storage or retrieval system, without the written permission of the Authors and Publisher.

Copyright © 2024 Iain McCartney
All rights reserved
ISBN: 978-1-915975-09-6

July 22nd 2024 saw the final spotlight extinguished, plunging the stage into complete darkness, as the curtain began to slowly close. There was no round of applause, although a standing ovation would certainly have not been out of place.

Abdul Kareem Fakir, better known to one and all as 'Duke' had announced, only a couple of days previously, that he had made his final performance as a member of The Four Tops, the last original member of the legendary quartet, known across the world for their extensive repertoire from Motown and beyond. However, retirement for the eighty-eight-year-old did not last long.

The Motown record catalogue is awash with many memorable introductions which when vibrating through the speakers, immediately penetrate the ear drums, capturing your attention. From the bass line of The Temptations 'My Girl' to the dance floor pulling opening salvo of The Elgins all-time classic 'Heaven Must Have Sent You' and the demanding 'Stop' from the nasally voice of Diana Ross.

Perhaps Berry Gordy could be considered a failure when it came to boxing or running a jazz-oriented record shop, but he knew the importance of the making the record buying public sit up and take notice of a previously unheard sound when it was played on the radio. He was a man who knew what he wanted and as he set off on his Motown adventure, he wanted The Four Tops.

He was to write in his 1994 autobiography 'To Be Loved': *"One of the acts I really wanted but had a hard time getting was The Four Tops. These four had been around for almost a decade. Already seasoned performers, they had been on the road with Bill Eckstine, and had played Vegas clubs. Their vocal blend was phenomenal. Their jazz-type harmony rang out in five parts even though there were only four voices. Smooth, classy and polished, they were big stuff. I wanted them bad."*

But forget those previously mentioned opening bars, those opening vocals, there was a more unforgettable moment to saviour, something almost spontaneous, words that are etched into the memory for ever, five words that, when heard are as instantly recognisable as any song ever recorded by The Four Tops.

"Just look over your shoulder", coming at two minutes thirty-eight seconds of the 1967 No.1 hit 'Reach Out I'll Be There', five words that catch the listener unaware, but five unforgettable words that were to become synonymous with the quartet, as were other memorable lines.

The Four Tops, however, did not have to look over their shoulders, there was no-one chasing them, no-one could get near them, no other group had a lead singer with a voice like that of Levi Stubbs. The Temptations could come close, but they required the mixture of vocals that their members could produce, whilst also needing to change their actual membership for various reasons. The Four Tops, however, remained solid. There was no behind the scenes problems. Levi Stubbs, Abul 'Duke' Fakir, Renaldo 'Obie' Benson and Lawrence Payton were a solid unit, life-long friends, all content in their position within the group. Although Levi often stood to one side, took the lead vocals on the majority of the recordings, they were a foursome, brothers in arms.

Only death was to bring enforced changes to the line-up in the modern era, but the crowds were still attracted, like moths to a flame, whenever the group were on tour and it is a flame that will never be extinguished, their legacy is a lasting one, thanks to the string of hits in their lengthy back catalogue.

What you are about to read within the pages that follow is not a definitive biography. There is no complete discography, which would force a book in its own, it is simply something that hopefully fills a void in the soul music book shelf and is appreciated for what it is, a tribute to the group, paying homage to the four guys from Detroit whose songs are always to be found on personal playlists [for me, nothing can beat that 'Second Album', a dozen tracks of pure excellence] and those of radio stations, with the odd recording to be found in a DJ's record box, which will drag the masses onto the dance floor.

So, thanks go to The Four Tops for giving us the memories and thanks to you for buying this book.

IAIN McCARTNEY 2024

ACKNOWLEDGEMENTS -
Marc Taylor [A Touch Of Classic Soul]; Sharon Davis; Jim Donohue; Chris O'Leary and the websites – worldradiohistory and Discogs

The Detroit of the immediate pre-war years was an industrial sprawl, the undoubted automobile capital of the word, encompassing the manufacturing plants of the Ford Motor Company, Dodge, Packard. Chrysler and Durant's, the latter having been behind the production of General Motors and Chevrolet. With jobs aplenty, it was not surprising to see a mass migration from the south to Michigan, with an estimated 400,000 arriving between 1941 and 1943, increasing its population from around 500,000 in 1910 to over 1.8million in 1950. This in turn raised racial tension as the city became a volatile mixture of colour, creed and religion.

Looking for not simply employment and better living conditions these new immigrants, a high percentage of whom were of African-American descent, were eager to escape the 'Jim Crow' laws of the southern states and although Detroit was far from being free of the intense, often intolerable day to day hatred that had transpired elsewhere, the city offered them a new lease of life along with the opportunity to raise a family in a comparatively safer and healthier environment. For many who had endured the often impoverish conditions in the southern states of America, the likes of Detroit took on the mantle of the promised land.

The majority of the new city residents were to make their homes on the east side of the city in what was called the Brewster projects, encompassing the neighbourhoods of Black Bottom [was there a pun intended?] and Paradise Valley [yet another possible pun]. Although incomparable to, let us say, New York's Manhattan or London's Knightsbridge, it was, however, misconceived as having been something of a run-down area, but was in fact far from it, as the projects in general provided affordable accommodation for those countless families who had arrived in the city. Unlike some, it was certainly not an area you wanted to relocate from as quickly as you could, as back in the day, it was considered a "beautiful, clean and secure neighbourhood", where a strong community respect for everyone could be found. It was not, however, by any manner of means, all blue sky and sunshine, but for many, it was a far cry from where they had come from.

PERSHING HIGH SCHOOL

As time went on, with the ugly face of racism lessening, improvements were made and a greater tolerance towards the non-white faces was shown.

The likes of Manhattan and Knightsbridge in the U.K. were areas that the rich moved into, having made their money in whatever business had grabbed their attention, or perhaps which one indicated the quickest route to untold riches, but in the projects, there was little in the way of riches, not in a monetary sense at any rate, although there was certainly ambition amongst many who lived there, loads of it, coupled with the determination to succeed, climb the social ladder and prove to everyone that colour was and should not be a hindrance in any walk of life. However, not everyone would achieve their ambition, fulfil their hopes and realise their dreams.

Due to the influx of newcomers, a new generation of Detroiters were born, reaping the benefits of schooling and a home environment that did not involve having toil alongside parents and siblings on the plantation fields, and at schools like Pershing High and Northern High, friendships were forged. Friendships that would last a lifetime.

Pershing High School opened its doors in September 1930 and brought together two youngsters from the North end area of the city, namely Abudul 'Duke' Fakir [born December 26th 1935] and Levi Stubbles [born June 6th 1936].

The Fakir's lived in a single-family home nearer to Pershing High School, Duke, whose father had arrived in Detroit from Bangladesh, where he played sitar on the streets, via a short stopover in London where he worked as a cook to raise the money to enable the family to cross the Atlantic, had been immersed in music from an early age, from singing solos in his grandmother's church and playing drums. He got to know Stubbs in his pre-teen years as they moved, often stealthily, around the same neighbourhood, the Stubbs family living in Russell Street, before moving to Dequindre Avenue near Six Mile Road, across the street from a certain Mable and Willie John.

"My father was a foundry worker" Levi was to recall. *"He was a very hard labourer and just worked himself to death. In fact, he died in the foundry when I was twenty-two."*

Singing ran in the family, with his younger brother Joe also being regarded as a very talented vocalist and who was to go on a record with the likes of The Falcons, The Contours, The Originals and One Hundred Proof Aged In Soul. The brothers, however, were never to record side by side in a group.

Levi Stubbs was something of an all-round sportsman, but despite his prowess on the track and field, singing was what he enjoyed most and he would spend just as much time at the Paradise Theatre, Detroit's answer to the Apollo, as he did outdoors. "*I would skip school to catch the likes of Sonny Til and the Orioles, The Dominoes, Duke Ellington and Sarah Vaughan perform at the Paradise Theatre*" he was to recall in later years.

The Paradise and the Warfield Theatre were as familiar to him as the local parks, as he had performed there on the regular 'Amateur Nights' coming up against the likes of Little Willie John, his sister Mabel John, Della Reese, Sammy Ward and Jackie Wilson and although competition was fierce, they would fix things so that everyone took a turn at winning.

Levi, his 'Stubbles' surname soon to be abbreviated to Stubbs as it looked and sounded better, was to become good friends with Jackie Wilson, whom he would often watch perform at the Paradise, as he did likewise with other acts such as Frank Sinatra, and along with Willie John, they could often be found rehearsing at Jackie's house.

"*Jackie was a sort of mentor for Levi*" Lawrence Payton was to say and the pair would eventually join up as members of The Royals, although they were never to share studio floor space.

Performing in those 'amateur nights', both at the Paradise and the Warfield Theatre on Hastings Street were also to get Levi bookings, as he could often be found named as a guest singer, with the likes of Lucky Millinder's band and numerous others, and it was one of those appearances that saw Duke Fakir discover that his baseball buddy could sing.

One night, whilst sitting in the audience, Duke was taken in by the singing of this guy on stage and looking closely, he thought that his

THE PARADISE THEATRE, DETROIT

face was familiar from somewhere. Leaving his seat and moving closer to the stage, he was astounded to see that it was his neighbourhood friend.

Although still to bond and form a life-time brotherly alliance, Levi and Duke were to be there for each other back in those teenage years, Levi preventing Duke from having a broken Coke bottle thrust into his face following involvement with a local gang, while the roles were reversed when Levi found himself the target for revenge from that same gang dispute, with Duke preventing a knife welding attack on his friend.

As luck would have it, the pair were to end up at Pershing High School and it was here that a lasting friendship was formed, one that would see Levi move into the Fakir home, with a room in the basement, where singing together was simply something they did.

A few kilometres south at Northern High School, another friendship was blossoming between Renaldo 'Obie' Benson [born June 14th 1937] and Lawrence Payton [born March 2nd 1938], with the school itself having more than its fair share of students who would go on to make more than just a dent in the music business – Smokey Robinson, Pete Moore, who would join Robinson in The Miracles and Aretha Franklin, to name but three.

Benson, a happy-go-lucky sort of guy, who was to grow up in a more impoverished area of which he was to say "was more like a ghetto", was determined to make something of himself and get as far away from those early surroundings as possible, hence his studying to become an architectural engineer and playing semi-professional basketball. On the music front, he was able to play trombone and cello.

As for Payton, who was raised by his grandmother Amelia Lee, along with two brothers and his cousin, Roquel 'Billy' Davis, at 557 King Street. He was to grow up in a devout, religious environment, singing in church and on street corners, while the family home would often vibrate to the sound of music as Lawrence's uncles would play the guitar and sing gospel.

Music was soon to unite Payton and Benson and they began singing together in a makeshift group called The Morals.

Although attending different schools, the four teenagers knew each other and 1954 was to see Duke and Levi receive invites to a 'Farewell to Pershing' party thrown by a group of girls who could be classed as coming from Detroit's black high society.

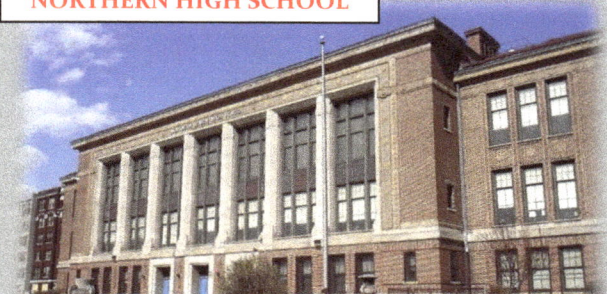

NORTHERN HIGH SCHOOL

The girls, debutants at the annual Cotillion Ball, were also singers, having a group called Scheherazade and they fancied a challenge against the invited duo who were known locally as good singers.

In order to level the playing field somewhat, Payton and Benson were recruited, the foursome sweeping the girls aside with their unrehearsed harmonies as they combined to wow the crowd with their rendering of the Roy Hamilton hit 'I'm Gonna Sit Right Down And Cry Over You'.

The die was cast and it was more or less decided there and then that the quartet should remain together and look towards obtaining regular bookings around the city.

Rehearsals became part of their regular routine with songs recorded by the likes of The Orioles, The Four Freshmen and Ray Charles enthusiastically learned and before long, dressed in matching suits, they were winning amateur talent contests at the Warfield Theatre on Hastings Street, Detroit and another at the Ebony Lounge in Cleveland, Ohio, earning the applause of the audience and the foursome a mouthwatering, at the time, $300. There were, however, dark clouds on the horizon. Fakir had been offered a basketball scholarship at Central State University, Ohio, while Benson had also been offered a college scholarship.

Plans were made for the quartet, who were now calling themselves The Four Aims, to perform during the summer months, then take up the college position in the autumn. Things, however, did not go according to plan, as the pull of performing in front an audience and reaping the applause was so great – *"once we hit that stage, we knew we were not going to college"* said Fakir and it mattered little if they were out there singing one night a week or seven, this was what they wanted to do.

At times, there was also a fifth 'Aim', with Roquel 'Billy' Davis often stepping up on stage, whilst also acting as the groups un-official songwriter and manager.

Speaking countless years later, Davis was to say of the fledgling foursome, that Lawrence had great ears and could hear the chords, while Duke was the tenor and could almost sound like a girl. In regards to Obie, he was the baritone, although Lawrence could actually sing lower than him, but Obie was the groups anchorman who enabled the other three voices to blend together.

He was also to add that the group did less dancing than the others found on the scene, as they didn't want to be considered like all those others who were around at the time, adding that their sound was not unlike that of some of the white doo-wop groups, with their close harmonies, but they were already a class apart due to their all-round singing ability.

From being nothing more than four guys who wanted to sing, they suddenly found themselves signed up with an agency – Twas & Casablanca.

With an agent now behind them their career gathered momentum and the now christened Four Aims were out to justify their initial ambitions of aiming for the top.

Under the management of Davis, a three-night appearance at Eddie's Lounge in Flint, Michigan, opening the show ahead of 'shake dancer' Tequila Wallace, earned the foursome the heady sum of $200, less the agency's fee of $50, less a further $50 to cover the cost of new suits.

The money was secondary to the applause that vibrated from the appreciative crowd, following their rendering of 'Work With Me Annie', 'September In The Rain' and 'How Deep Is The Ocean'.

Booking followed booking and their reputation continued to grow, but they needed to judge themselves alongside other acts, see where they could improve and what had still to be polished to take them to the next level. That opportunity occurred when they journeyed south to unknown territory in Atlanta and the Royal Peacock Club. If travelling into the deep south wasn't nerve wracking enough, then having to follow a certain James Brown on stage was enough to test the most seasoned performer, never mind four still relatively wet behind the ear's youngsters.

Watching from the side of the stage, as Brown held the audience in the palm of his hand, steadily cranking up both the audience and the atmosphere to a different level with every song.

ROQUEL 'BILLY' DAVIS

Following the master would be a severe test. On the other hand, they had nothing to lose.

Having dragged out the interval to allow the audience to regain some form of normality, Stubbs was later to say: *"We can't out-funk him. We can't out-dance him. We can't out-holler him, but we can out-sing this motherfucker. So, we are just gonna go up there and sing...Come out there singing and looking debonair and just sing to the ladies. That's all we can do. That's us."*

'This Can't Be Love' with Obie taking lead, was followed by Levi out-front on 'How Deep Is The Ocean' and what followed was enough to secure them not simply the attention of the crowd, but their applause which was immensely gratifying considering their unknown status.

Looking to emulate the famous Mills Brothers, their repertoire could switch from jazz to standards with more than relative ease, a huge plus as it would secure them the sought for bookings at numerous different venues, in particular those around Detroit where they were beginning to establish a sizeable fan-base.

If there had to be a year that was to kick-start the careers of the four Detroit friends then few would argue against 1956, as not only did it mark the first, and only, venture into the recording studio as The Four Aims, laying down their only known release under that moniker - '**If Only I Had Known**' b/w '**She Gave Me Love**' which was reputedly issued on the Grady label [012]. It was also to bring about the name change to the

one they would be universally known as for the foreseeable future.

Their repertoire back then was little more than standards, things like The Dominoes 'Sixty Minute Man' and the Frank Sinatra/Four Aces recording 'Three Coins In The Fountain', but they could turn their hands to anything, hence the numerous doors that would open for them, with distance being no object. Summer seasons were also amongst the continuous, seemingly never ending, list of bookings, as they were signed up by Arthur Bragg as part of his Idlewood Revue.

Idlewood was a black resort, near Baldwin, Michigan, popular with Detroiters. There was never a shortage of big names on the bill, from Jackie Wilson to T-Bone Walker, Arthur Prysock to Della Reese, Choker Campbell to The Falcons. It wasn't exactly akin to Butlin's, but like many who wore the distinctive red coats, it was an ideal springboard to bigger and better things.

"If we would make a mistake in the show, Arthur would have us rehearsing that particular thing over and over again for two or three hours the next day."

It certainly did the Tops no harm to enjoy prolonged contracts under Bragg as it was to earn them not just an appearance on Broadway with the Larry Steele Revue, but a countrywide tour with the black vaudeville type show.

For the group, Idlewild was also a heaven on earth with a readily supply of food, drink and women, in particular the Ziggy Johnson Dancers, with three of the quartet, Duke, Obie and Levi meeting their future wives

Being paid for doing something that they loved was a bonus, while hearing the applause from their appreciative audience was equally rewarding, as was the knowledge that if the latter was forthcoming, then the monetary rewards would follow.

There was, however, no substitute

to performing live, with recording work coming as an added bonus, their own meagre attempt to date, coming to nothing. But they were back in the studio, working with Maurice King and the Wolverines, the in-house band leader at Detroit's Fame Show Bar supplying the backing vocals for Carolyn Hayes on her 1956 Chateau release **'Baby Say You Love Me' b/w 'Really'** [Chateau 2001] which was quickly followed by similar four-part harmony vocals on the Dolores Carroll recording **'Everybody Knows' b/w 'I Just Can't Keep The Tears From Tumbling Down'** [Chateau 2002].

Their work with Maurice King, who was to alert the group to the name clash with The Four Aimes, bringing about that change of name, was an ideal learning curve, while their association with Davis saw him send demos of three recordings - 'All My Life', 'Could It Be You' and 'Kiss Me Baby' to Chess Records.

As it was, Chess was well endowed with male vocal groups, already having The Moonglows and The Flamingos under contract, but what they did not have were writers of the calibre of Billy Davis, so, in order to get one, they had to take the other. However, in reality the winners were the label and Billy Davis who penned the hits 'A Kiss From Your Lips' for The Flamingos and 'See Saw' for The Moonglows.

From The Four Tops perspective, they gained the valuable studio experience, if not hits, recording eight tracks for Chess on April 4th 1956, with only two seeing the light of day – **'Could It Be You' b/w 'Kiss Me Baby'** [1623] in late May, both penned by Billy Davis.

Of the 'A' side, the 'Cashbox' review read – *"The Four Tops combine in good style as they chant the middle beat rhythmic number with a cute romantic lyric. The boys are looking for the right girl who possess all the qualifications. Good deck, well done."*

In regards to the 'B' side review – *"The Four Tops turn out a fast beat rocker with all the enthusiasm the item demands. Good treatment, except that the embellishment has already adorned other recordings."* This side was given a 'B', while the 'A' side received a 'B+'.

That 'B' side was to surface again in 1987 amid the Beach Music boom, issued on the

Ripete label on the album 'Shagger's Delight Vol. 3', considered as something of a stand-out R&B track – a rarity in The Four Tops vast discography, with a reviewer mentioning that it was surprising to hear such harmony coming from the group.

The others, **'I Woke Up This Morning'**, recorded at the same session was never given a catalogue number, but eventually appeared via the Hip-O-Select released Street Corner Essentials [314 556 264-2]. **'Country Girl'** was to later appear on the Chess 'Rhythm and Roll' – cd boxset. **'I Wish You Would'** can be found on 'The Best of Chess Vocal Groups Volume 1' CD. **'All My Life',** again recorded in 1956 appears on the album 'The Chess Rhythm and Blues Collection' released almost twenty years after it was recorded. Two other unreleased tracks were **'I'm My Baby's Sitter'** and **'More Than A Friend'**. All are worthy of a listen today.

For the anoraks, there was also an unreleased recording of a duet of 'All My Life' with this particular take featuring Davis and Stubbs.

According to Duke Fakir in regards to Chess Records, *"If we had gotten a hit, they would've given us a deal."*

Davis and the Tops were on the road between 1956 and 1958, doing one-nighters in the black clubs of the Southern states, along with the predominantly white dance clubs. Some nights failed to produce the agreed fee, seeing them almost stranded miles from home.

Out on the road, an appearance in 1958 at the Thunderbird in Las Vegas, brought the usual appreciative applause from the enthusiastic audience, but it was also to attract the attention of legendary jazz recording artist Billy Eckstine, who was so impressed that he signed them up as the opening act for his forthcoming nationwide tour.

Billy Davis had by now, left The Four Tops for good, teaming up with a guy called Berry Gordy, the duo going on to pen various hits such as 'Lonely Teardrops' and 'Reet Petite' for Jackie Wilson. Gordy had, however, bigger dreams than penning a handful of hit records, but as the sixties appeared over the horizon, all he had were

dreams, as there was no record label for Davis to persuade his partner to sign his four friends to, something that was to prove a stumbling block, although Gordy would not have required much in the way of persuading as he already knew all about the quartet, having heard them on numerous occasions in and around Detroit and he wanted them as part of his on-going plans.

Gordy made contact with the foursome, explained what he had planned and that he wanted them on board. Many would have seized the opportunity with both hands, but not these guys. *"We were not only reluctant to sign"* said Duke Fakir, *"We didn't want to. The possibility of a black company making it was very obsolete. We were already thinking big. We just didn't think he had a chance."*

Although used with getting his own way, Gordy simply shrugged his shoulders and both parties got on with their ambitions.

So, instead of joining forces with the novice Gordy and his still to be established record label, The Four Tops were to accept a four-record deal with the long-established Columbia Records, signing for John Hammond the same day as a promising young female singer called Aretha Franklin,

Neighbourhood friends in Detroit, the Tops, or The Four Aims as they were back then, had encouraged the teenage Aretha to form her own group, which she named The Cleo-Patrettes, whilst also trying to tempt her to follow their path to Chess Records, but she was already connected, through her father, to JVB Records.

Always happy to help others, but those early Detroit days for the group were hard, a lot of the time they didn't get paid, while according to Levi: *"Sometimes we*

only ate two meals a day. Often our supper was a pound of ham, split on four rolls." Lawrence Payton was to add that one night in Cleveland dinner was "*a couple of cans of sardines and a bottle of grapefruit juice.*"

As the sixties began to blossom, Columbia were certainly at the forefront of issuing records in a 45rpm format, whilst being able to boast as having the legendary jazz quartet of Duke Ellington, Louis Armstrong, Dave Brubeck and Miles Davis amongst their rota of artists. They could, however, do nothing with the quartet from Detroit and The Four Tops were only to see one release on the label '**Ain't That Love**' b/w '**Lonely Summer**' recorded in the spring of 1960, the former penned by Levi Stubbs, who also managed to claim publishing rights to the track.

In their issue of August 13th 1960, Cash Box looked upon the recording favourably – "FOUR TOPS (Columbia 41755) (A) "AIN'T THAT LOVE" (2:22) [Levi Stubbs BMI—Stubbs] R&B-flavored team bows on the label with a happy-beat blueser. Team has a fine teen spirit.
(B) "LONELY SUMMER" (2:48) [Merrimac BMI — Kosloff, Kasha] Item gives the crew a chance to

display its rock-ballad wares, and it comes-across with sincerity."

Columbia Records, however, was simply nothing more than a brief flirtation, there was no major promotional effort from the label and they were released from their contract by mutual consent.

Two years down the line they were back in Detroit setting down tracks with a couple of small labels – Red Top and Singular, but their studio work, whatever it consisted of with those two labels, was never to see the light of day.

Two tracks from back then that did see release came out on the New York based Riverside label – '**Pennies From Heaven**' b/w '**Where Are You**' with the Cash Box issue of December 1st 1962 carrying the following review – "THE FOUR TOPS (Riverside 4534) "PENNIES FROM HEAVEN" (2:30) [Joy BMI-Burke, Johnston] The old timer goes the teen route in this lively Latinish cut from the song crew and its instrumental accompaniment. Enough sparkle here to create interest in the deck among the kids.

As for the 'B' side - "WHERE YOU ARE" (2:24) [2nd Sound BMI-Keyes, Smith, Jones] In much more subdued showing, the guys display a somewhat jazz blend on a pleasing romantic."

Both sides were given a 'B' by the reviewer, which translated into 'Good'.

The previous week, Billboard had listed the Bert Keyes produced 'Where You Are' as the 'A' side, but gave no comments as to the disc's credibility, simply giving both sides three stars. But three stars and a 'B' did not guarantee chart success.

1962 did not see that double-header release from Riverside, conjure up another of those *"sign on the dotted line and we will produce a couple of records and see how it goes"* deals, and there were further recordings made on Red Top and Singular, both local Detroit labels, but again there were to be no commercial releases.

Although unperturbed by their lack of success recording wise, something that certainly did not affect their bookings across the country in any way, the boys began to cast envious glances across Detroit where Berry Gordy was beginning to gain a foothold in the record market. Jazz was Berry

Gordy's taste in music, but it had proved to be his downfall when he stocked his record shop with such records, paying little heed as to what the local record buying public wanted.

The Four Tops, or perhaps more to the point Levi Stubbs, was also heavily influenced by jazz, and as a quartet, they felt quite at home sharing a stage with the likes of Dinah Washington, a huge favourite of Gordy's, in the summer of 1963 at the prestige 20 Grand night club in Detroit.

Gordy, whilst swooning over Dinah Washington, was equally captivated by The Four Tops. They were no strangers to the would be record label mogul, as he had of course attempted to sign them whilst they were with Columbia but The Tops were not overly impressed. *"He came to us and asked us if we wanted to be part of his company. We flatly refused — we didn't think a black guy had a chance of making big strides in the record business.*

"Maybe we were too hasty in shunning Gordy when he approached us."

It was a topic that often popped up in conversation, which in turn lead to a discussion about trying to get back in touch.

Summer had been and gone, the leaves were falling off the trees and Gordy's Motortown Revue was at the Apollo Theatre in Harlem and if the guys needed an elbow in the ribs, then this was the night, as they sat watching from the audience and to be taken in by professionalism of a highly polished quartet and certainly far more experienced than their soon to be stable mates. They were also just as well known locally as those contracted to Gordy's label. Only the lack of any chart success left a gap in their more than impressive CV.

Facts can get intermixed with fiction over the years, but one story tells of Gordy's desperation to get the group on board that he sent out his A&R man Mickey Stevenson with the instruction to find them and bring them to 2648 West Grand Boulevard.

Stevenson stuck to his task and rounded up the quartet and they duly arrived in Gordy's office. Although both parties were equally relieved to sit face to face again, things did not quite go as planned,

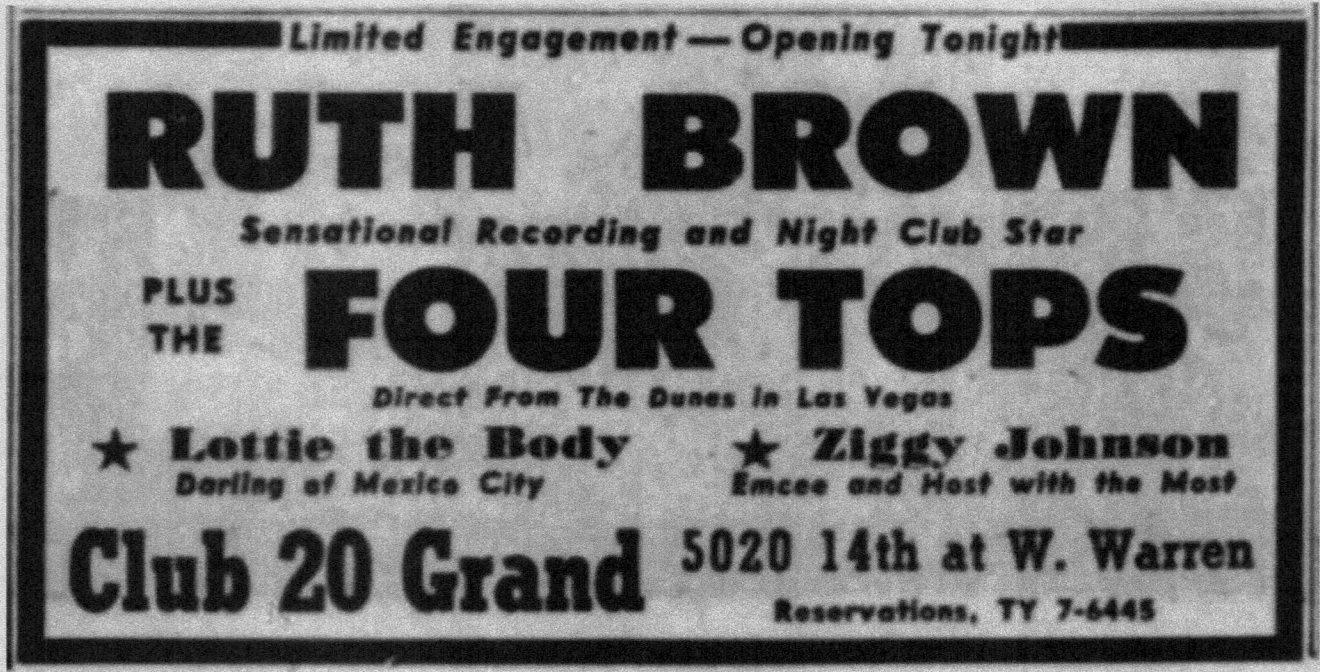

to no avail. This was despite not simply having achieved chart success with The Miracles and their single 'Shop Around', but having a number one hit on the Billboard R&B chart, number one on the Cashbox Top 100 Pop Chart, and number two on the Billboard Hot 100 chart, giving the group and Gordy a million-selling hit record with that 'Shop Around' single. those appearing in front of them, The Miracles, The Contours, Martha and The Vandellas, Stevie Wonder and Marvin Gaye. *"We went and saw that and said, Wow, they are good!"* recalled Duke Fakir, *"We need to be there"*, although in reality, those Motown acts on the bill could not in reality, hold a candle to Levi, 'Duke', Obie and Lawrence, as they were already certainly not for Gordy.

Pulling a contract from his desk drawer, he simply pushed it forward, telling the foursome to sign on the dotted line. He was, however somewhat taken aback when he was told that they were going to take it away with them and study it before signing. Stunned by the request to take the contract home, Gordy simply replied that it

good and knew we could work, but all we were doing was getting enough money to get by. We weren't doing what we wanted to do. We wanted to get into the masses, and we knew we needed him in order to do that. They promised us hit records; that's basically what he promised. That's why we signed it. He said: "I'll get you hit records. Don't worry about that."

Asking to take the contract home was something of a risk on the group's behalf, but it was one they were prepared to take and it paid off as Gordy, for perhaps the only time, relented. Not only that, when he was asked for an advance, he simply shook his head at their audaciousness, but then handed over $400. *"We were a little disappointed about that"* commented Fakir, *"but it wasn't about the money."*

Now that Berry Gordy had The Four Tops signed to Motown, it was simply a case of what to actually do with them. They were far from those raw youngsters who had made their way through the door at West Grand Boulevard, as they had a decade of experience behind them, having played with a host of big-name acts, at equally big venues, travelling the length and breadth of the country in doing so.

There was certainly no instant success as bookings were centred around the local night clubs, while early studio work was as backing singers for anyone and everyone. *"For a couple of years we sang on practically every Motown record that was put out. You name it, we were on it,"* said Lawrence Payton.

Receiving actual label credit for such work was few and far between, although 'What Goes Up, Must Come Down', a rare Eddie Holland/Lamont Dozier recording does credit them and The Andantes.

Eventually, Gordy did get them to record **'Get My Hands On Some Loving'**, a Marvin Gaye/Mickey

was not something that he did. *"We had been out there, so we knew a little bit about record deals,"* said Duke Fakir. *"The kids, they didn't know anything. We had been through two or three record deals. We took it home and looked at it and decided we were going to sign regardless of what was on there. We needed a record. We knew we were

Stevenson track that Gaye had recorded for his 'That Stubborn Kinda' Fellow' album, while it was also covered by The Artistics, but in the cold light of day, Gordy was of the opinion that it wasn't the Four Tops sound he was looking for so decided against releasing it.

It was eventually to appear in May 2005 on 'Lost Without You' - 1963-1970, Hip-O Select - B0003626-02

Meanwhile, Gordy was still deeply engrossed in jazz, whilst being of the opinion that in order to get the general record buying public on board, perhaps better defined as the older record buying public, he had to give them tunes they were familiar with whilst at the same time tempt them with his ever-growing rota of artists offering a completely different type of music. So, instead of putting his newly signed quartet onto one of his already established labels he assigned them to his Workshop Jazz subsidiary.

Although more than competent, not to mention comfortable with the type of music that Gordy required for the album, it took the guys around a year's studio work between April 1963 to May 1964, to complete '**Breaking Through**' [WS217].

The outcome, however, could be considered as nothing more than a waste of time, as the album was to see no commercial release despite acetates and a sleeve produced. Needless to say, those acetates command exceptionally high prices with collectors, while rumour has it that a few copies of the album were produced, with one said to have sold for $800 in 1980.

The album did eventually see daylight in September 1999, re-packaged as a '**Lost And Found: Breaking Through'** in a CD format – [Motown – 012 153 365-2].

The tracks, in the sequence that they were recorded in were - '**Fascinating Rhythm'**, '**Stranger On The Shore', 'I Left My Heart In San Francisco", This Can't Be Love', 'I Could Have Danced All Night'**, laid down on April 19th 1963; '**Young And Foolish'** – April 21st; '**Every Day I Have The Blues'**, '**Can't Get Out Of This Mood'**, '**On The Street Where You Live'** – May 25th; '**Until I Met You'** – May 25th/June 1st; '**When**

I'm Alone I Cry', '**If My Heart Could Sing'** – June 22nd; '**Gee Baby Ain't I Good To You'**, '**Maybe Today'** – October 9th; '**Nice And Easy'**- October 17th; '**Discovered'**, '**End Of A Beautiful Friendship'** – May 15th 1964. There was also a bonus track – '**I'm Falling For You'** recorded live at The Apollo with Billy Eckstine on Augus 14th 1965.

One track planned for the original album 'The Night We Called It A Day' did not appear on the CD version, despite its existence on acetate with the only explanation given as that of the harmonies being a "bit off".

The album is arguably far removed from the groups familiar style of latter years, but the jazzy harmonies were in the direction that Lawrence Payton saw the group taking, or perhaps more to the point, wanted the group to take. He was to feature as lead on 'Stranger on the Shore', 'Get Out of This Mood' and 'Maybe Today', while Obie Benson stood to the fore on 'This Must Be Love', while Levi Stubbs got his share of the limelight on seven of the eighteen tracks.

"The Four Tops were never a doo-wop group like The Temptations," said Billy Davis. *"So, in order to make them more commercial they had to showcase the lead singer. The other three Tops agreed to do harmonies to a lead voice. Lawrence was still responsible for the vocal arrangements.*

"There were a few phrases that they sang collectively; at other times they sang straight harmonies behind Levi, which was sometimes augmented with an orchestra, horn players from Maurice King's band and available Detroit Symphony string players."

Perhaps left disillusioned, the guys must have wondered if they had indeed made the right choice in signing for Motown, but their doubts were washed away when Gordy, having initially informed them that he felt the 'Breaking Through' album was *"Not commercial enough. It's good, but I don't think we can sell it right now"*, announced that he was going to pair them off with three guys who he considered would be ideal to work alongside and who he was certain would help them achieve that much sought after hit record. Step forward Eddie and Brian Holland and Lamont Dozier.

In the meantime, it was session work as backing singers in the studio and back on the road playing at various venues, but it wasn't for long.

The story goes, that following one gig at the famed 20 Grand night club in Detroit on May 7th 1964, the sweat stained quartet had barely come off stage when an enthusiastic Brian Holland came into the dressing room and declared "I've got that song", proceeding to play a piano version on a tape recorder. "That's pretty good" came the response to which Holland replied that he wanted them down at the studio right away to record the track while they were still in the mood following the show.

Following a show in Amsterdam, Duke Fakir was being interviewed by a journalist from the 'New Musical Express' and related something a little different: *"We were over at Marvin Gaye's house having a party, when suddenly, we all got the urge to make a record. We got on the phone at 4.00am and called various musicians and sound engineers. By 5.00am we were at the Tamla studios and singing our hearts out for an hour. Then we went back to the party."*

When asked the name of the record that was the result of that particular session, he replied that he couldn't remember, but Levi would know, "as he knows everything". "It was Baby I Need Your Loving" came back the instant reply.

Recording at night was nothing new at Motown, as there always seemed to be a sound engineer on site, plus the early hours of the morning were a more than ideal time to claim the studio for recording purposes.

Just to clarify, the backing track was recorded by Holland-Dozier-Holland on April 10th, with the Tops adding their vocals to the arrangement a month later on May 7th, with the 'B' side recorded three days later.

Issued in the States on July 10th 1964, 'Cash Box' reviewed the track in their issue of July 25th with the following – *"**BABY, I NEED YOUR LOVING** (2:43) [Jobete BMI-Holland, Dozier, Holland] **CALL ON ME** (2:33) [Jobete BMI-Holland, Dozier, Holland]. Watch for the Four Tops to step out in their next big attraction from the Tamla/Motown set-up. Artists' Motown bow is an intriguing rock - a-cha-cha beat pleader, dubbed "Baby, I Need Your Loving," that they carve out with solid sales authority. Undercut's an inviting beat-ballad romancer."*

It was soon to be a regular inclusion on the play lists of the R&B DJs, but despite its familiarity with the listeners, it just missed out on a top ten placing, although it did remain in the listings for three months, making number four in the R&B charts, but across the Atlantic it was to be an entirely different matter altogether.

Released in the UK on the Stateside label, it was reviewed somewhat briefly in 'Disc' on September 19th 1964, simply appearing in the 'in short' reviews, amongst names likes The Chants, Jerico Brown, The Gonks and Danny Delmonte, while The Applejacks, Susan Maughan, Jackie Trent, Timi Yuro and Major Lance had their names in large bold letters in the main review section. Basically, The Four Tops were amongst the 'also rans'.

Going by the review only, it is doubtful if it would have attracted much attention on this side of the Atlantic - *"Another from Tamla Motown. Mixed group noise from boys and girls on a flowing item. Baby I Need Your Loving – very smooth. Call On Me is a slow contrast. Bluesy and well led by a boy who sings it as if he really does love the girl."*

The 'Record Mirror' was equally scathing in its review in the issue of

the same time, with the record once again relegated to the 'Singles In Brief'. Its review read: *"Fast rising U.S. hit. Jaunty but disjointed vocal delivery on a not so commercial song. Probably too way-out for here."*

The latter review simply sums up how Motown in general was perceived by the British record industry, although the humble 'Rugby Advertiser' classed it as *"a typical US-style disc.*
"It's a finger-snapper with much orchestration."

Praise of a sort I suppose.

But for the group themselves, it was what they had yearned for over the course of a sweat-stained, tiring decade, covering thousands of miles playing gigs across the length and breadth of the country.

When the dynamic trio of Holland-Dozier-Holland took their latest project into the Hitsville studio, they decided to experiment by extracting Levi Stubbs from the quartet and placed him out front, the lead singer in other words, with his friends immediately behind, supplying what was basically backing vocals. It was something that the boys had never really implemented previously, as they were content slipping effortlessly in and out of taking the lead throughout their vast repertoire.

Stubbs, however, had that gritty, distinguished vocal, but had to be coaxed into using it to its maximum effect by Lamont Dozier, something he did not quite appreciate and suggested that the lead should be given to Lawrence Payton. Dozier, whose vocal range was considered similar to that of Stubbs, would have none of it and along with Eddie Holland, finally managed to persuade Levi that he had the vocal range to accomplish what was required.

Eddie Holland was equally enthusiastic about the recording. "*I was excited about it because I had heard about The Four Tops in my teens. Levi was one of the most significant and greatest singers that I'd ever heard, and the Four Tops as a group had some of the best harmony that I had ever heard. One of the things that stood out was that Duke Fakir has a very beautiful and distinctive first tenor voice, which added to the richness of their sound.*"

That enthusiasm certainly didn't stretch as far as the quartet themselves.

"*We weren't overly excited*" Duke was to confess later, "*We were excited because it seemed like they [H-D-H] were working toward getting us a hit. The song was just good. It wasn't something that made us jump out of our pants. When I heard it on the radio two weeks later... I jumped out of my pants. The mix was just awesome.*"

Eddie Holland was also to recall that when they initially gave the song to Stubbs who, having taken the tape home, returned to the studio and said that he didn't have a real feel for the song., but he had never really rehearsed it and that it was different from what he had been used to singing.

With Stubbs finally convinced, the recording was set up, with The Andantes brought in to hit the high notes, an octave above the guys.

If 'My Girl' was to become The Temptations 'national anthem', then 'Baby I Need Your Loving' in turn was to become The Four Tops counterpart.

The British music scene in the late fifties, early sixties was awash with plagiarism and it isn't an exaggeration to say that every group or individual artist was guilty of it, although only a few came out with any credit for their cover versions of the original American produced recordings. This was certainly the case when The Fourmost made the decision to record 'Baby I Need Your Loving'.

When played on the popular BBC television programme 'Juke Box Jury', three of the four panellists were scathing in their comments relating to record on the grounds of its "similarity and cover approach". Gene Pitney, however, went as far as to suggest that the Fourmost version was better.

Annoyed at the rejection, the band were quick to respond and in an interview for 'Record Mirror', Fourmost Billy Hatton hit back with: "*The situation quite simply is this. The Four Tops disc came out weeks ago and despite a heck of a lot of plugging it just didn't do much on sales. We waited, deliberately, to give the Americans a chance to make it - or not make it. We liked the song. In fact, it was easily the best we'd heard in a long time. If John and Paul had come up with a better one. O.K., we'd have done that.*

"*But it IS a big song and it needs a backing. That's where this 'copying' allegation comes in.*

"*We used a big orchestra and choir. Our recording manager, George Martin, said we needed this sort of sound - and we accepted his word. After all, he's had a lot of hits . . .*"

Fellow group member Brian O'Hara waded in with: "*Anyway, people who say we've copied the Tops should actually listen to the discs. We've cut a lot out on the main phrases - and the string backing is definitely better on our version. Sounds a bit dodgy for us to say it, but we reckon our disc is more commercial as far as Britain is concerned.*"

It was to reach number twenty-four in the charts, although Peter Robinson, who reviewed records in his 'Pop Scene' column of the 'Worthing Gazette' was to call the Fourmost version as being an "unbelievably inferior amateurish cover job", mentioning that the Tops version received little air-play except on Radio Caroline.

In those mid-sixties, Motown was akin to the conveyor belted automobile plants scattered through Detroit, where Berry Gordy had toiled on a daily basis, notebook and pencil in his back pocket, scribbling down what he envisioned as being lyrics for future hit songs. One session would be finishing on certain artists, while others stood behind the closed doors waiting on their turn behind the microphones.

Due to that constant stream and the number of recordings, it was clearly obvious that not all would see the light of day, with those "rejects" of the Friday meetings that decided what was or wasn't released being confined to shelf space in the vaults, never to re-surface until a number of decades later.

One such track was '**Gotta Say It, Gotta Tell It Like It Is**', originally written for Marvin Gaye, and it was to see the vocals laid down at that same 'Baby I Need Your Loving' session. It was not until May 2005, however, that it finally received an airing on the 'Lost Without You' CD, along with countless other tracks.

With 'Baby I Need Your Loving' still in the charts, albeit on the way down, the Tops were back in the studio at the beginning of October, laying down what was to be their follow-up single '**Without The**

But Jopling wasn't alone when shouting from the roof tops in regards the groups output, as the regional newspapers once again had their fingers on the pulse, not surprisingly in the likes of Liverpool where 'Disker' in the 'Liverpool Echo' of January 9th 1965, having sang the praises of Mary Wells a few paragraphs earlier penned the following in regards to 'Without the One You Love' – "*The Four Tops (Stateside) continue to be one of the lesser-known Tamla Motown units so far as British audiences are concerned. Sales of their last single were stunted by the Parlophone cover version of "Baby I Need You Loving" made by The Fourmost who are still hovering somewhere in the mid-twenties of the hit parade with the number. "Now The Four Tops are out with "Without The One You Love," another spirited big-sounding arrangement which opens with the title-line of "Baby I Need Your Loving" and retains a similar flavour throughout. Some of the lyrics are lost in an overcrowded accompaniment but the over-all effect is impressive."*

Another regional newspaper, the 'Melton Mowbray Times' saw 'Sylvia' write: "*The Four Tops are not a very well-known group as yet, but may become more popular when their new release "The One You Love" has a few more hearings. This is a very good arrangement that really keeps your interest. I doubt if anyone will sleep through it, anyway."*

The failure to make a real impression on the charts was, to say the least, disappointing. So much so, that Gordy shoved them towards his head of A&R Mickey Stevenson

One You Love' b/w 'Love Has Gone', which saw release Stateside the following month and in the UK January 1965.

The track was certainly not as strong as that initial release, but it did receive favourable reviews in the two main American music publications – 'Billboard' - "*FOUR TOPS - WITHOUT THE ONE YOU LOVE (LIFE'S NOT WORTH WHILE) (Jobete, BMI) (2:51) - Here's a hot group right in the commercial groove with wailing hot-pop, r&b song. Tremendous beat and excellent performance. Flip: "Love Has Gone" (Jobete, BMI) (2:50). Motown 1069*" while in 'Cash Box' – "*WITHOUT THE ONE YOU LOVE (2:51) [Jobete BMI - Holland, Dozier, Holland] LOVE HAS GONE (2:50) [Jobete BMI - Holland, Dozier, Holland] FOUR TOPS (Motown 1069) The Four Tops, who scored heavily with their Motown chart bow, 'Baby, I Need Your Loving' can quickly duplicate that success with this new stand. It's a feelingful jumper, tagged 'Without The One You Love (Life Is Not Worthwhile),' that the fellas carve out in very commercial fashion. 'Love Has Gone' is a complete change of pace beat - ballad heartbreaker. Both Holland & Dozier produced sides are in the boys new LP.*"

In Britain, however, many were beginning to latch on to R&B, sending letters to the UK music papers deriding the blatant copying and "mutilating of original American recordings", but there was no shouting from the rooftops, although Norman Jopling, who was to do much for the cause on this side of the Atlantic, did give that follow-up to 'Baby I Need Your Loving' a favourable review in 'Record Mirror' in January 1965. – "*FOUR TOPS: Without The One You Love; Love Has Gone (Stateside SS 371), A fair hit in the States, this group vocal pushes along on a typically feelingful Tamla Motown production. Nice ideas mid-way with a compulsive backing. Outsider for the charts.*"

An outsider for the charts it certainly was, as it was just to make the lower reaches of the Top 50 in America, which in reality meant that there was little hope of it breaching the UK charts no matter what Norman Jopling thought.

along with Ivy Jo Hunter for the follow-up single.

Putting their heads together and again, as Lamont Dozier had done, pushing Levi Stubbs back into what was basically a solo role, they created the haunting, show stopping ballad '**Ask The Lonely**' b/w the Holland-Dozier-Holland '**Where Did You Go**'. Once again, the other group members supplemented by The Andantes and backed by a soaring string section, created a song of awesome proportions which emphasised the lead singers vocal ability as he tugs at the heart strings of the listener.

If 'Baby I Need Your Loving' is the Tops national anthem, then this beautiful, atmospheric side is the ultimate show stopper, with Levi Stubbs at his very best – *"They'll tell you a story of sadness, a story too hard to believe. They'll tell you the loneliest ONE is me. Just ask the lonely. Ask me...."*

"*Levi could sing his but off*" said Duke Fakir. "*His voice just did things with lyrics that made you feel it. The lyrics just came alive to you. He lived those words when he was singing them. You could hear it in his voice. I think it was Levi's voice more than anything and the way he delivered that song that gave 'Ask The Lonely' its appeal.*"

Appeal it certainly had, although 'Billboard' simply mentions it as a new release, without any actual review. However, the same could certainly not be said for the record reviewer in the pages of the 'Sevenoaks Chronicle and Kentish

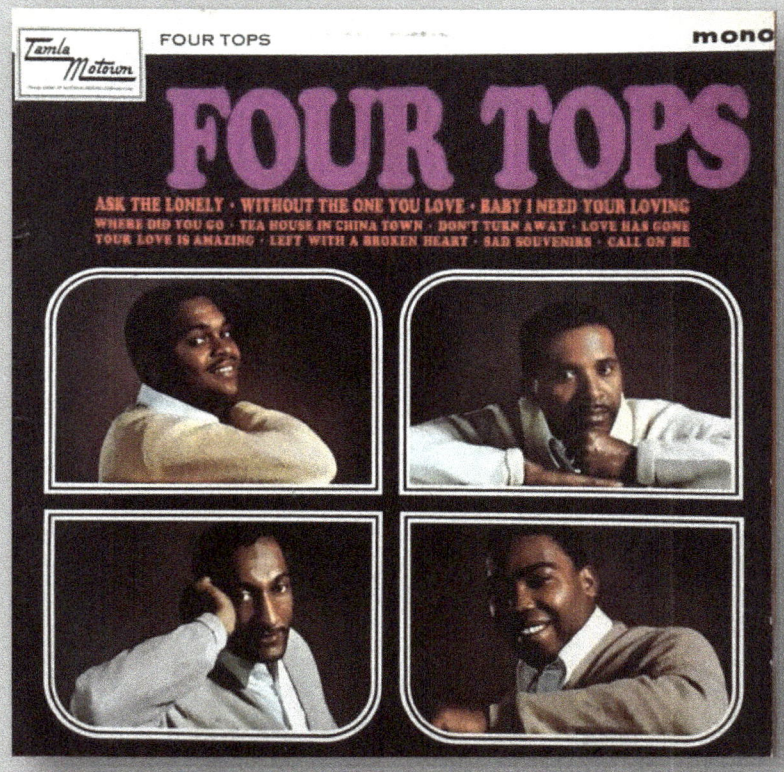

Advertiser', who may well have been little more than an office junior, as their issue of Friday April 2nd 1965 carried the following: *"On the new Tamla Motown label. The Four Tops come on to the scene with "Ask The Lonely" and "Where Did You Go." A really good record this one. It boasts talent, quality, and class, and is one of the second batch of "single" releases on E.M.I.'s new label. On this showing, The Four Tops will be on the "pop" scene for a long time to come."*

Equally complementary, once again, was Peter Robinson of the 'Worthing Gaztte' who wrote in 'The Pop Scene' section of the April 7th 1965 issue of the newspaper: *"But my own personal favourite is by the Four Tops, the group who brought us the original soulful version of Baby, I Need Your Lovin'. Their new single, Ask The Lonely, has a terrific powerful sound, with the mood set by a chanting chorus and shimmering strings. Then the lead singer launches in with his unique vocal style. The song is really moving, possibly one of the best Motown releases ever. And that's really saying something!"*

Much credit should be given to people like Peter Robinson and the other reviewers in, let's say, small local newspapers compared to the national dailies, as they helped do their bit in the promotion of records such as 'Ask The Lonely'.

Written and produced by Mickey Stevenson and Ivy Hunter and released in January 1965, 'Ask The Lonely' deserved to do better chart wise - it failed to make the pop top twenty in 'Billboard' by four places, although it was a song that would remain in the groups set list through to the present day.

Close on the heels of 'Ask The Lonely' in mid-January 1965 came the release of that initial LP, simply entitled '**Four Tops**' and in all honesty it would have done little to grab the attention of the UK public,

perhaps not even that of their American counterparts, as it simply contained their three singles to date – 'Baby I Need Your Loving', 'Without The One You Love' and 'Ask The Lonely' along with their relevant 'B' sides. The remainder was little more than fillers, 'Your Love Is Amazing' aside, with 'Tea House In China Town', something of a flashback to what would not have been out of place in their stage show of a few years back. The others were 'Sad Souvenirs', 'Don't Turn Away', Marv Johnson's 'Left With A Broken Heart', 'Love Has Gone' and 'Call On Me' featuring Lawrence Payton on lead.

From being at the forefront of 'Baby I Need Your Loving', Levi Stubbs was returned to his more familiar, and favoured, position alongside his fellow group members for 'Without The One You Love', but this was only temporary as 'the voice' of The Four Tops was soon to be thrust back to centre stage, as that blue touchpaper was ignited and the rocket was finally soaring upwards.

With the effervescent sixties now well into its stride, there were many like the Norman Jopling, a scribe with the 'Record Mirror', who were beginning to take considerable interest in black American music, but the days of Chuck Berry, Howlin' Wolf, Bo Diddley, Sonny Boy Williamson and company as being the main men were numbered.

London was becoming the pop music epi-centre, fan produced publications were also beginning to appear – 'Rhythm and Blues Gazette' having surfaced in June 1963, with 'R&B Scene', a more professional looking publication following towards the end of 1964, both leaning towards the Blues, while Motown continued to find its feet.

But that was to change in March 1965, when Gordy decided that it was time to broaden the horizon and take his artists across the Atlantic, kicking off the twenty-four days, twenty-one twice nightly shows at the Finsbury Park Astoria on 20th March 1965.

It was, however, to be a tour without The Four Tops and The Temptations, although the latter had flown in simply on promotional business. If Levi and co. were disappointed, they never let on, and in any case, they would soon be making the journey across the Atlantic to a greater reception than the tour itself managed, as it more often than not played to sparsely crowded theatres.

The failure of 'Ask The Lonely' to attain that chart success could be attached to the fact that the music scene was continuing to change, night clubs that were now playing records rather than promoting live acts were beginning to blossom, while teenagers were creating a similar environment within their local youth clubs, dancing rather than simply listening to records there and at home.

If they wanted to dance, then the next offering by the Tops was certainly right up their street.

Despite the in-house rivalry, the Motown acts were always very supportive of each other and it was a night at the 20 Grand that sowed the seeds for the next offering from the group.

Back in Detroit, enjoying a night away from performing, Levi, Duke, Lawrence and Obie were to be found, along with Lamont Dozier, at the 20 Grand Night Club, watching The Temptations, when right out of the blue Dozier casually

mentioned that he had an idea for their next single.

Once the show had finished everyone headed back to Lamont's house where he sat down at the piano and played the basic tune.

Phone calls were made and soon the Motown studio was alive with what was to become '**I Can't Help Myself**', which would be backed with '**Sad Souvenirs**'.

"*It was two in the morning before we even heard the song*" Levi Stubbs was to recall. "*When we recorded it, I felt there was nothing to the song. Eddie Holland sat me down and said Levi, sing the song, I guarantee it will be a big hit for you. I didn't believe him.... Shows you what I know.*"

It was after the second take that Levi announced that he wasn't happy and he wanted to go through the song again. Much to his annoyance, Brian Holland told him it was fine, but he could come back to the studio the following morning.

Determined to go through the song again, Levi duly turned up at the studio only to be told that there was no time slot available. Whether this was known to Holland previously matters little, Levi was left disappointed and the previous night's recording of 'I Can't Help Myself (Sugar Pie Honey Bunch)' was now in the can.

As time would tell, Levi Stubbs was proved wrong, again, in his assessment that the song needed re-working, while the more trained ear of Brian Holland once again proved correct, as the record, led by James Jamerson's bass line is regarded as the song that kick-started the Motown success story, the song that defined what was to become 'The Motown Sound' more than any other. "*That's one of the most famous riffs I came up with*"

Lamont Dozier was later to say. "*It's probably one the most well-known bass figures there is. Everybody's done it.*"

Released on April 23rd 1965, Billboard' considered it something of "*a spirited, fast-paced wailer performed in their unique style*", while the 'Cash Box' reviewer was to call it "*A rollicking hand-clappin' thumper about a fella who is delighted 'cause he's head-over-heels with the gal of his dreams*". The 'B' side, 'Sad Souvenirs' was seen as a "*tradition-oriented effectively building bluesy tale of rejection.*"

On this side of the pond, it was reviewed as resembling the Supremes 'Where Did Our Love Go' in the 'New Musical Express' with the added comment "*It's the usual Motown treatment of male soloist, chanting support, tambourine, handclaps and an irresistible beat*".

That irresistible beat took in to the top of the 'Billboard' discotheque charts by the end of June, whilst enjoying a nine week stay at the top of the publications R&B charts, whilst also claiming the top slot on the Hot 100 chart, earning the accolade of being the biggest R&B single of the year and the second biggest in the Hot 100 singles of 1965.

Good old Peter Robinson of the 'Worthing Gazette' was once again on the ball, writing in that newspapers issue of Wednesday May 19th: "*I hear that the great Tamla Motown group The Four Tops are making their first promotional tour to this country very shortly, which accounts for their new release, I Can't Help Myself, so soon after their superb Ask The Lonely. It is a pity that they should come to plug this, since all three of their previous Tamla singles are much better, especially Baby, I Need Your Loving. The new song has their distinctive sound, with solo lead vocal and the others supporting him, and a string-dominated orchestral accompaniment. The beat is pounding, and the melody line vaguely like Where Did Our Love Go?"*

The release of 'I Can't Help Myself' did bring Levi, Duke, Lawrence and Obie across the Atlantic to the UK for the first time, promoting the single with appearances on 'Ready Steady Go' on Friday May 21st 1965 [described in the 'Daily Mirror' as being nothing more than "an American Tamla-Motown group"] appearing alongside The Who, and on 'Thank Your Lucky Stars' the following Saturday, when they featured alongside Billy Fury, The Nashville Teens, The Rockin' Berries, The Who, again, and Connie Francis amongst others.

The popularity and general appeal of 'I Can't Help Myself' is perhaps best acknowledged with the fact that in that Top 100 chart, having replaced The Supremes 'Back In My Arms Again', it was deposed by The Byrds 'Mr Tambourine Man', only to bounce back like a championship boxer and regain that top spot, before being replaced for a second time by The Rolling Stones 'Satisfaction'.

Satisfaction there must have been for Levi, Obbie, Duke and Lawrence, all that hard work over the years finally paying off bring its deserved awards. Many, however, have achieved similar success and then found themselves unable to maintain that momentum, sliding back into more or less obscurity. That was not an option for the Four Tops, nor were Holland-Dozier-Holland going to make them little more than one-hit wonders. They all had reputations to maintain.

There was, however, like that of their fellow Motown acts, still some considerable work to be done in an effort to find acceptance in Britain, although that initial breakthrough was announced in the 'New Musical Express' of July 9th 1965 – *"Four Tops In At 22 – Everyone can be a fan"*, with the brief accompanying article saying: *"One of the most versatile groups from the Motown stable, the Four Tops are as much at home singing country and western numbers as they are with modern jazz."* A week later, it had peaked at number 23.

For those in the UK who knew little or nothing regarding The Four Tops, 'Record Mirror' brought them up to date in an interview in October 1965.

Speaking in regards to their live performances, Levi Stubbs explained *"We feature country and western, rock and roll, straight pop and vocal harmonies from Lawrence Payton. That's our modern jazz section.*

"People that go to night clubs want to hear most types of music. In theatres you get nine-to-thirty-year-olds. Pop stuff for them. You know what to give your audience."

Stubbs was also to say that they didn't take recording seriously prior to arriving at Motown *"as I guess the song writers weren't groovy enough. Tamla have their own songwriters. They produce something then it's sorted around until one or other of the artistes records it. Often a song is treated many ways before it's finally decided who it'll go to."*

He was to add that financially, things had improved, while there were added perks such as a series of dates on the Playboy Club circuit *"and who'd moan about that."*

But before moving on, there might well have been an even bigger hit appearing within the Four Tops discography than that of 'I

Can't Help Myself' had Holland - Dozier - Holland managed to get their way.

With those immaculate and unforgettable vocal tones of Levi Stubbs in mind, the dynamic Motown trio penned 'This Old Heart Of Mine'. There was, however, a stumbling block, a big one, in the form of Berry Gordy. Having recently added the Isley Brothers to his ever-growing roster of artists, he wanted an early hit from the trio, something in the way of payback towards his investment and insisted that 'This Old Heart Of Mine' was the track for the new boys at Hitsville.

Did Levi get the studio time to wrap his voice round what is still a floor-filler today? Quite possibly, it could either be gathering dust somewhere or has disappeared altogether, never to be seen or more unfortunately never heard.

Having noticed the impact that their former contracted group were creating, Columbia re-issued 'Ain't That Love' in mid-1965 but they were to be disappointed, as it was more or less over-looked by the record buying public, only reaching No.93 in the Top 100 and they were to find themselves out of pocket at the end of the day, as Berry Gordy, upon learning about the planned re-issue made contact with the President of Columbia Records and asked him to pull the record. The suggestion was ignored, so Gordy retaliated by cancelling the production of Motown records at Columbia's West Coast manufacturing plants.

1967 was to see 'Aint That Love' and 'Lonely Summer' surface once again, on a CBS various artists compilation - 'Soul Sounds', which also featured tracks by Shirley Ellis, Peaches and Herb and Aretha Franklin.

Back on home turf, however, the lights were on full spotlight mode. 'I Can't Help Myself' was quickly

followed by the pounding 'It's The Same Old Song', released in July 1965.

Berry Gordy never appeared to stand still, always on the move and as soon as one of his records hit the top ten, never mind the top of the charts, he was on to the artist, writers and producers to get that follow-up recorded. And so it was with The Tops and 'I Can't Help Myself'.

During one of the more than occasional card games, Gordy cornered the group and their now writing team of Holland-Dozier-Holland and asked what the follow up would be. *"We don't have one came the reply"*. *"Well get to work and find one"* fired back the boss.

That follow up was to materialise, like many others, simply out of the blue.

Having spent yet another night at the 20 Grand night club, Duke Fakir and Lamont Dozier were enjoying a nightcap at the home of the latter when Dozier began messing about on his piano and began playing 'I Can't Help Myself'. He suddenly switched to playing the melody slightly differently, catching the ear of Duke Fakir who immediately exclaimed *"That's 'I Can't Help Myself' backwards."* *"Yeah, I know"*, came the reply, *"it sounds like the same old song"*. The pair left it at that and Fakir went home.

The following morning at the Motown studios, the Holland's and

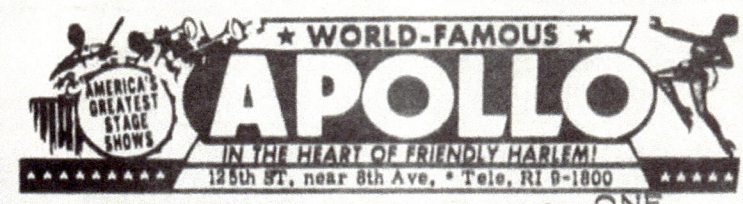

Lamont Dozier called the Tops in and said that they had the follow up ready for them to record. Upon hearing it, Fakir simply looked at Dozier and exclaimed "you son of a bitch", equally bemused when he was told that the track was called '**The Same Old Song**' b/w '**Your Love Is Amazing**'.

According to Fakir in a later interview, he was to say that following the recording, *"Brian Holland mixed it the same night. The next day it was on acetate and the boys were stamping the labels. Monday morning it was on the radio and Monday afternoon it was in the charts."*

In his 2009 book 'Tamla Motown – The Stories Behind the UK Singles' Terry Wilson states that chief engineer Lawrence Horn was instructed to set up the studio for 3.00pm, the lyrics were then written for a backing track that had lain dormant since May.

The first take was done at 5.00pm with the rest of the night spent on mixing and over-dubs, followed by 300 promotional copies being cut in-house.

The following afternoon, one and a half thousand copies had been pressed and sent out for distribution to DJs etc. and twenty-four hours further down the line, the record was in the shops and selling.

Released in July 1965 and backed with 'Your Love Is Amazing', all the music paper reviews were positive, although it failed to emulate its predecessor as it only hit the number two slot on the Billboard R&B chart and number five in it's Hot 100. In the UK, it failed to hit the Top Twenty, managing only a lowly thirty-four.

Berry Gordy sensed that he was on a good thing with The Four Tops, urging them back into the studio as soon as one record began to move slowly down the charts, leaving little breathing space between hits, with **Something About You** b/w **Darling I Hum Our Song** released towards the end of October 1965, making it four hits in that year, spiralling the Tops into an in-demand quartet who would feature regularly on national American TV, with appearances on the likes of 'Hullabaloo', 'Shindig!', 'Where The Action Is' and 'The Ed Sullivan Show'.

Choreography had aways played an important part of their stage shows and it was their appearances in front of the cameras across the States that projected what was to become their signature move – swinging from the waist, with arms up-stretched and palms raised.

"*'Something About You' - The tune is a rollicking, fast-moving, romantic rocker about a lucky lad who is on cloud number nine since he met the girl of his dreams*" was the opinion of the Cashbox reviewer, adding that *"Darling, I Hum Our Song' is a tender, slow-shufflin' tradition-oriented blues weeper"*.

It hit the US charts at No. 67 at the beginning of November 1965, rising a further sixty places on the Billboard R&B charts.

The 'New Musical Express' of December 3rd 1965 was to review 'Something About You' as *"An altogether more raw and earthy sound. The nagging and insistent heavy beat has a hypnotic effect. Not so tuneful as The Supremes disc [I Hear A Symphony – reviewed a couple of lines previously], but it's the atmosphere that counts."*

That same week, the 'Record Mirror' saw it as a 'Top Fifty Tip' with the reviewer saying: *"Certainly good enough for the charts – this one shows off a more way-out side of the group, who've nibbled, chart wise before. Lead voice starts off a riff-ish song with massive backing sounds, and then the vocal group sound comes through strongly. It has a sort of immediacy of appeal that should give strong chart placing."*

There was one other review and this one perhaps hit the nail firmly on the head. It appeared in Dave Godin's 'Hitsville' No. 10 and read: *"Hard driving and with a droning riff supplied by rasping saxes and the slightly rasping voice of Levi taking lead, this is a winner all the way. Compulsive and catchy it will become a classic in time."*

Indeed, a classic in time, as of all The Four Tops single releases, this is the one that has stood the test of time above all others as it remains a firm favourite today on the Northern Soul scene, with the opening bars being enough to see a surge onto the dance floors. It couldn't, however, emulate 'The Same Old Song' or 'I Can't Help Myself' by making an indent in the British hit parade.

With their popularity at an all-time high, hard on the heels of their four hits, Motown pushed out '**The**

Four Tops Second Album', released November 1965, and for this writer, even taking out 'I Can't Help Myself', It's The Same Old Song' and 'Something About You', this is the ultimate Motown album, Hitsville at its very best, or perhaps that should read, Holland-Dozier-Holland at their best, as all but one of the dozen tracks are written and produced by the trio. The odd man out being 'Is There Anything I Can Do', a Smokey Robinson produced number, co-written with his fellow Miracles Ronnie White and Warren 'Pete' Moore.

Many LPs are fashioned around two or three hits, with the remainder taken over by nothing but fillers. Ok, this album contains the 'B' side of 'It's The Same Old Song ' – 'Darling I Hum Our Song' but the remainder – a cover of the Kim Weston recording 'Helpless', along with 'I'm Grateful' and 'Since You've Been Gone' would have the toes tapping, while 'Stay In My Lonely Arms', also covered by The Elgins, 'Is There Anything That I Can Do', Just As Long As You Need Me', 'I Like Everything About You' and another Lawrence Payton led track 'Love Feels Like Fire' can certainly not be considered as fillers. Excellent stuff. Many, however, considered that the best was yet to come.

If 'Something About You' had failed to appease the British record buying public, the follow-up **'Shake Me, Wake Me'** b/w **'Just As Long As You Need Me'**, released in February 1966 was also unappealing to many despite its No.5 placing on the Billboard R&B chart.

Many were of the opinion that the British music papers often paid little heed, or in some cases completely ignored American R&B, into which category Motown was nudged, so much so that the early to mid-sixties began to see the 'home produced' fanzines raise their head and their importance should not be ignored.

In regards to 'Shake Me, Wake Me', the Tony Cummings edited 'Soul' was to review the record as being *"From one of Berry Gordy's most consistent groups, this drives along in typical Four Tops fashion, with plenty of pounding percussion and big band backing. The tune is complex but has a hint of ''Same Old Song'. Exciting listening. The flip's quite good too. All Tamla addicts should have this by now, if not, buy it at once."*

Some four months after 'Shake Me, Wake Me' came the release in July 1966 of the Ivy Jo Hunter/Stevie Wonder penned **'Loving You Is Sweeter Than Ever'** b/w **'I Like Everything About You'** – considered *"an off-beat blueser"* in Billboard, it was to reach only No.12 in their R&B top twenty.

Reviews in the U.K. were once again favourable in the regional press, with Peter Murray in the 'Staffordshire Sentinel' penning: *"Swinging Tamla beat introduces "Loving You Is Sweeter Than Ever" recorded by The Four Tops. This Tamla Motown single (TMG 568) is fabulous for dancing. The lead singer is joined by the rest of the group chanting the lyrics like an echo after his voice. Big orchestral backing. Could find its way into the charts."*

Find its way into the charts it did, but only in the Top 40, reaching a disappointing No. 21.

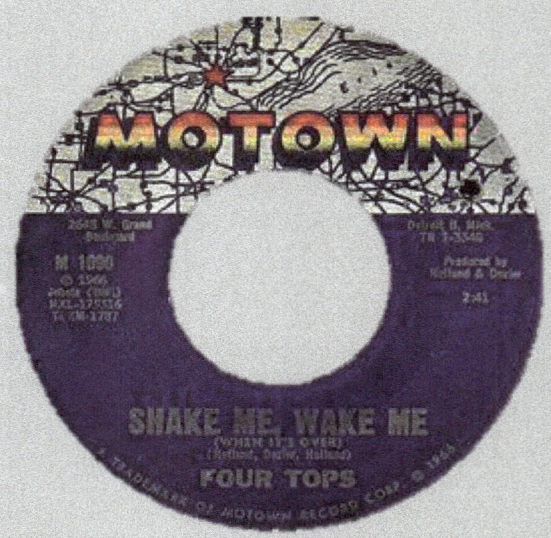

Hot on the heels of those two singles came the groups third album, simply entitled '**On Top**' released in July 1966.

Placing the needle at the run in to the opening track, the listener was immediately hit with the pounding 'I Got A Feeling' before the pace was quickly lessened by the captivating Eddie Holland penned 'Brenda', the track appearing as the 'B' side to his 1963 Motown recording 'Leaving Here'.

This was followed by the groups two previous single releases, which in turn were followed by 'Until You Love Someone' and 'There's No Love Left' to close side one.

In regards to side two, it was to see the quartet drift back to something that could be considered their supper club circuit set list and once again, it took a review in a Dave Godin publication, this time it was his 'Rhythm & Soul USA', to hit the nail firmly on the head. If it was Godin himself who wrote the review, he certainly didn't show any bias, simply telling it like it was –
"*Like the curate's egg, this album is excellent in parts, but being so diversified it is hard to know at what market exactly it is aimed at. Half of the LP consists of their recent hits, which as you will all be aware, are solid examples of the Detroit Sound at its best, but the other half sounds like a big mistake, for, far from being the 'Sound Of Young America', it is more the sound of the middle class Copacabana set, and sounds more suited to the Workshop rather than the Motown label.*
"*Their jazz interpretations of number like 'In The Still Of The Night' (which is not the Five Satins number), and 'Michelle', etc, are not really likely to appeal to R&B fans nor are they likely to appeal to jazz fans (who would not associate their name as jazz singers), and thus this album falls between two stools and is hardly likely to achieve*

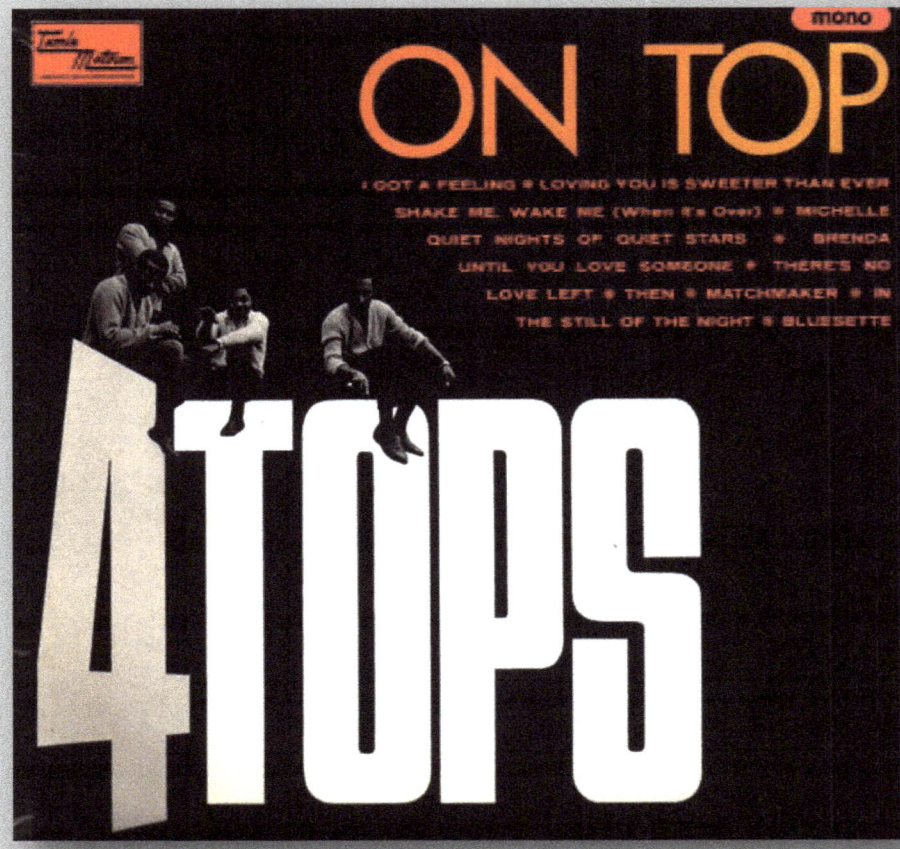

that much desired goal of pleasing everybody. There is not really a lot more that one can say, except that it is slightly disappointing.
"*Not their best.*"

It was an album that would most probably have seen side one played considerably more than side two, but it was one that continued to emphasise just how versatile the group were.

Although they were not only versatile and having emerged as the biggest name in Berry Gordy's growing recording business, there were no airs and graces about the quartet, who were more than happy to venture into the studio on days when they were not scheduled to be recording and supply backing vocals to anyone who needed them.

"We were the male voices behind many of the early Marvin Gaye recordings," said Lawrence Payton. "We liked to call that time as our apprenticeship in Motown. Whatever they needed us for, we were there. I remember standing right next to Eddie Kendricks, like it was yesterday, singing for other acts."

Lawrence and his fellow Tops can also be heard alongside The Andantes on the Mickey Stevenson/Ivy Hunter production 'My Baby Loves Me' recorded by the Vandellas-less Martha Reeves and alongside Holland-Dozier-Holland on The Supremes 'When The Lovelight Starts Shining Through His Eyes'.

Payton was also to mention in a 'Billboard' interview that he "*taught The Four Freshmen-type of harmony that the Tops specialised in to many others in Motown, including Marvin Gaye and The Temptations.*
"*We sang four-part harmony; that was our trademark. We used to sing*

'I Left My heart In San Francisco' and when we got down to the end, we put a tag on it and went up real high."

When it came to promoting not just Motown, but black American music in general, to the often-fickle British public, one name tends to stand out above all others, that of Dave Godin. His enthusiasm for the music extended way beyond simply listening to and buying the records, introducing many others to the sounds being recorded on the other side of the Atlantic, as he had begun putting his thoughts down on paper by producing the 'Mary Wells and Motown News' back in December 1963.

The seeds were sown and from there, Godin launched the 'Tamla Motown Appreciation Society' which in turn lead to Berry Gordy sending a number of acts to Britain for the first time for that previously mentioned tiring and poorly supported tour.

Godin was to re-vamp his five-issue Mary Wells publication, re-launching it as 'Hitsville USA' and in issue No. 4 – April 1965 came their initial introduction at any length to the British public, with a two-page article which included a

review of their first album.

The following quote, un-credited to any member was also included: *"We are inspired by anyone with talent. We watched the biggest stars because they are always the best."* Having been asked why they spend so much time working on their stage act, when they could get away with just going on stage and singing, the reply was *"People see us on stage and expect us to do something like the Monkey, but when we do something smooth like 'Nice and Easy', they sit up and really pay attention because we have a special routine for that!"*

The following issue of Hitsville, No.5 from May 1965 carried the first message from the Four Tops to their fledgling British fan-base.

There were to be concerts, club appearances, simple promotional work via television and radio, but performing on stage under the lights was on the horizon.

The music of black America, R&B, Soul, call it what you like and include Motown in that, was plagiarised without any degree of shame by the majority of both the professional and the often-abysmal amateurs scattered the length and breadth of the U.K.

Although they set a bench mark within the U.K. music scene, The Beatles were as guilty as any, recording versions of Barrett Strong's 'Money', The Marvelettes 'Please Mr Postman' and The Miracles 'You Really Got A Hold On Me' – all on the album 'With The Beatles'. Not to mention, Chuck Berry's 'Roll Over Beethoven', Arthur Alexander's 'Anna', The Cookies 'Chains', The Shirelles 'Baby It's You' and 'Boys' and The Isley Brothers 'Twist and Shout' on their first album 'Please, Please Me'.

They perhaps escape with a lesser sentence than some for their plundering by taking Mary Wells on tour with them in 1964, although it is arguable that only a few, outside the ranks of the connoisseurs, along with Dave Godin and his clan would be overly familiar with her. It could be argued that The Beatles played a very minor part in introducing Motown to the masses, but if that can be considered as being correct, then their manager, Brian Epstein could be regarded as being instrumental in giving it a major boost, picking up where that ill-fated tour left off and brining The Four Tops to the U.K. to perform exclusively at London's Saville Theatre on Sunday November 13th 1966.

The recent British television appearances would have whetted the appetites and on the back of their string of hits, Epstein's timing was excellent, with the promoter unperturbed to the Tops relative inactivity in the UK charts and if some thought it to be a gamble, then they were quickly proved wrong, with many left wondering just why there had not been more success on this side of the Atlantic for the band. More so, when it was announced that due to the "fantastic demand for tickets" they would now play an additional performance at 6.30 pm, prior to the previously advertised 8.30 pm one.

Not one to miss out on something good, Epstein flew to the States prior to those Saville Theatre performances and signed the quartet up for a major ten city tour in January/February 1967 taking in Southampton, the Royal Albert Hall, London, Liverpool, Leeds, Newcastle, Glasgow, Sheffield, Manchester, Birmingham and Leicester.

Epstein's timing in regards to both the Saville Theatre concerts and the forthcoming tour was uncanny, as he was to receive the ultimate boost that any promotor or artist could wish for, in the form of a number one hit.

The failure of 'Something About You', 'Shake Me, Wake Me' and even 'The Same Old Song' to make a substantial impact on the U.K. charts was disappointing to say the least. Something was required and quick. Gordy and Motown were not known for standing still and personal awards such as 'I Can't Help Myself' being voted the top R&B single of 1965 and the group themselves being voted the top male vocal group of 1965 had to be equalled.

Not having penned 'Loving You Is Sweeter Than Ever', Gordy informed Brian and Eddie Holland and Lamont Dozier that they would be responsible for the next Four Tops single.

Putting their heads together, they were to come up with 3.01 timed recording of what is considered to be not simply a triumph for the talented Holland-Dozier-Holland trio but the pinnacle of The Four

Tops recording career and one which always features in any top ten of Motown's greatest ever records.

That song was '**Reach Out I'll Be There**' b/w '**Until You Love Someone**'.

"When we recorded 'Reach Out' I didn't pay any attention to it and neither did Levi" Duke Fakir was later to say. *"He just said how Brian had him singing and talking in this particular song. We didn't think anything of it.*

"Berry called and said "I want to have a meeting with you guys."

He called the meeting and we sat down and he said "I really would like for you to call your accountants and make sure all of your finances are really in order. I don't want you to run into tax problems. I'm about to release the biggest record you ever had."

"I said bigger than "I Can't Help Myself?".

"He said, "I think so."

"I said, "Well, when are we going to record it?"

"He said, "You recorded it already."

"Levi and I looked at each other and said, "Yeah? Well what is it?" He played it, and I said, "Oh Berry, c'mon, man, don't mess us up. We're on a roll and have it going. That's not going to work.

It's not us. Berry, please don't release that, it'll kill us.

"He said, "That's going to be the biggest record." "I said, I don't know man. I know y'all have been really picking records. Y'all are about to break your own record with this one. This won't even make the charts, Berry. "He said, "You gotta be kidding, Duke. This has already been cut and released.

"We walked out of that meeting pretty upset. We were really mad."

Within a fortnight, they were all

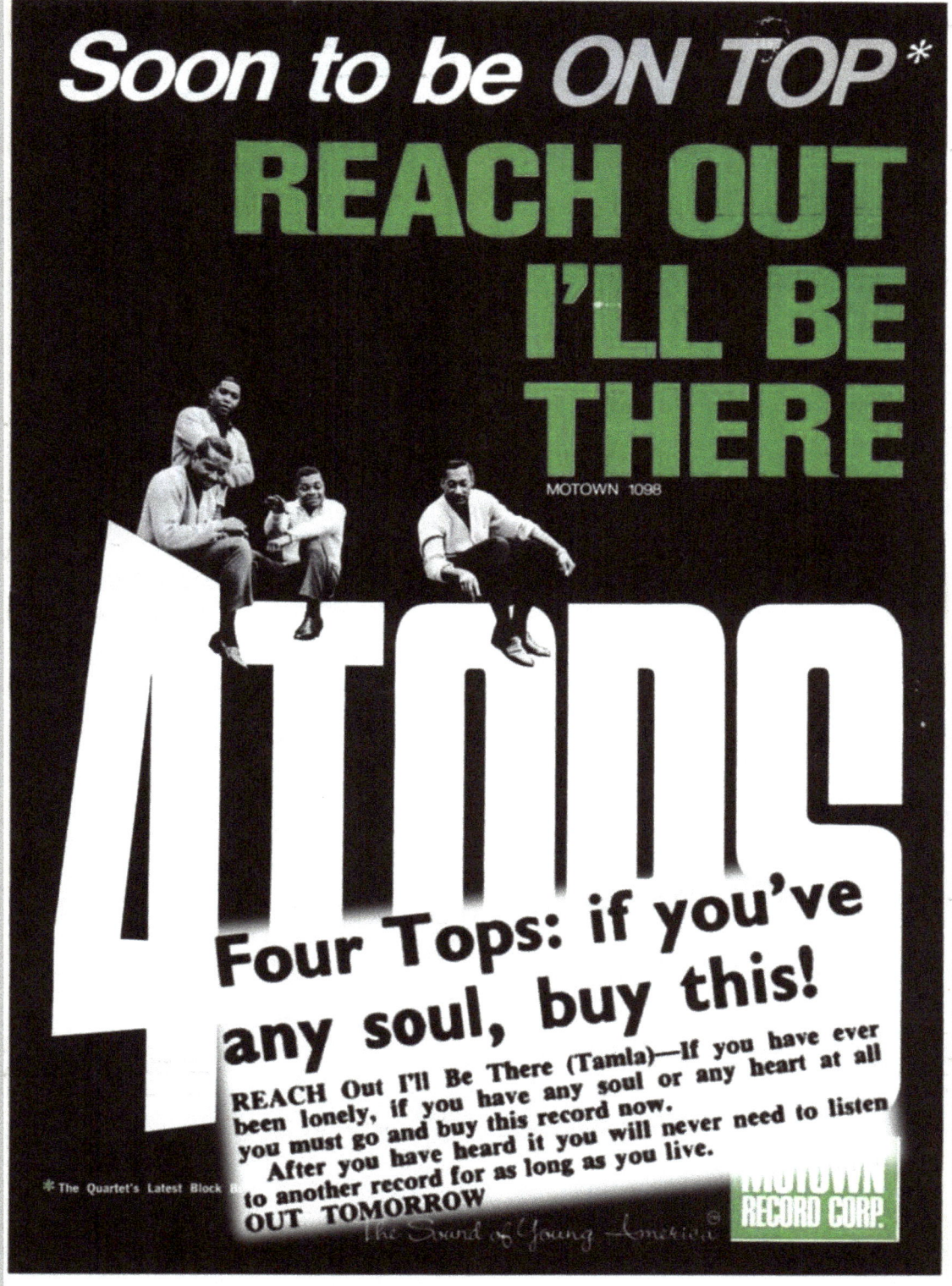

back in Gordy's office, only this time it was to make a humbling apology, as not only had the Tops changed their minds about 'Reach Out I'll Be There', the record was selling like hot cakes and bounding up the charts.

Gordy simply laughed, saying: *"We don't all hear everything. I would have missed a few myself if it hadn't been for Quality Control."*

From that opening instrumental introduction including the thirteen-year-old flautist Dayna Hartwick, to the seemingly off the cuff "Just look over your shoulder", the song had hit written all over it. Gordy was 100% correct.

But what of the record reviewers? Did they side with Gordy or the Tops?

'Cashbox' - *"The Four Tops' long hit chain should be still further enhanced on the basis of this latest Motown item. The 'A' side here, 'Reach Out I'll Be There' is a hard driving, pulsating pop-r&b romancer about a very-much-in-love guy who claims that he'll always be at his gal's beck-and-call. No flip side information available at press time."*

Just over a month later, it was ready to be launched on the British record buying public – *"Four Tops: If you've any soul, buy this! Reach Out I'll Be There (Tamla) - If you have ever been lonely, if you have any soul or any heart at all you must go and buy this record now. After you have heard it, you will never need to listen to another record for as long as you live. Out tomorrow"* – 'Disc and Music Echo'.

'Record Mirror' carried the following that same week - *"Almost oriental instrumental opening, then galloping hoof sound, then a fiery attack on a song which should be a substantial hit here. A strong arrangement, commercial song and*

TOP SELLING R&B SINGLES

Billboard SPECIAL SURVEY for Week Ending 10/29/66

★ STAR performer—Sides registering greatest proportionate upward progress this week.

This Week	Last Week	Title, Artist, Label, No. & Pub.	Weeks on Chart
Billboard Award	2	REACH OUT I'LL BE THERE — Four Tops, Motown 1098 (Jobete, BMI)	8
2	4	LOVE IS A HURTIN' THING — Lou Rawls, Capitol 5709 (Rawlou, BMI)	9
3	1	BEAUTY IS ONLY SKIN DEEP — Temptations, Gordy 7055 (Jobete, BMI)	10
★4	6	B-A-B-Y — Carla Thomas, Stax 195 (East, BMI)	9
★5	7	BUT IT'S ALRIGHT — J. J. Jackson, Calla 119 (Tamelrosa, BMI)	5
6	3	KNOCK ON WOOD — Eddie Floyd, Stax 194 (East, BMI)	10
★7	10	DAY STRIPPER — Vontastics, St. Lawrence 1014 (Maclen, BMI)	9
8	8	SAID I WASN'T GONNA TELL NOBODY — Sam & Dave, Stax 198 (East-Pronto, BMI)	6
★9	11	I WANT TO BE WITH YOU — Dee Dee Warwick, Mercury 72584 (Morley, ASCAP)	13
10	5	YOU CAN'T HURRY LOVE — Supremes, Motown 1097 (Jobete, BMI)	11
11	13		2
★12	15		7
13	14		
14	9		
15	12		
★16	22		
27	19	AIN'T NOBODY HOME — Howard Tate, Verve 10420 (Rittenhouse, BMI)	11
★28	32	SHAKE YOUR TAMBOURINE — Bobby Marchan, Cameo 429 (Tree) BMI)	4
★29	33	HEAVEN MUST HAVE SENT YOU — Elgins, V.I.P. 25037 (Jobete, BMI)	6
30	31	THE BEST OF LUCK TO YOU — Earl Gains, HBR 481 (Cal, BMI)	8
31	34	NEVER LIKE THIS BEFORE — William Bell, Stax 199 (East, BMI)	4
★32	37	I'VE GOT TO DO A LITTLE BIT BETTER — Joe Tex, Dial 4045 (Tree, BMI)	3
★33	38	I JUST DON'T KNOW WHAT TO DO WITH MYSELF — Dionne Warwick, Scepter 12167 (U.S. Songs, ASCAP)	3
★34	39	BANG! BANG! — Joe Cuba Sextet, Tico 475 (Cordon, BMI)	3

NME TOP THIRTY

FIRST-EVER CHART IN BRITAIN — AND STILL THE FIRST TODAY!

(Wednesday, November 9, 1966)

Last Week	This Week	Title / Artist	Highest Position / Weeks in chart
1	1	REACH OUT I'LL BE THERE — Four Tops (Tamla-Motown)	5-1
6	2	GOOD VIBRATIONS — Beach Boys (Capitol)	2-2
7	3	SEMI-DETACHED SUBURBAN MR. JAMES — Manfred Mann (Fontana)	3-3
		— Hollies (Parlophone)	5-2
2	4	STOP STOP STOP — Spencer Davis Group (Fontana)	2-4
		GIMME SOME LOVING — Paul Jones (HMV)	5-6
			12-1

Billboard HOT 100

For Week Ending October 15, 1966

★ STAR performer—Sides registering greatest proportionate upward progress this week.

				TITLE — Artist (Producer), Label & Number	
Billboard Award	2	7	10	REACH OUT I'LL BE THERE — Four Tops (Holland & Dozier), Motown 1098	7
2	1	1	1	CHERISH — Association (C. Boettcher), Valiant 747	8
3	3	6	8	96 TEARS — ? (Question Mark) & the Mysterians, Cameo 428	7
4	6	18	26	LAST TRAIN TO CLARKSVILLE — Monkees (Tommy Boyce & Bobby Hart), Colgems 1001	6
★5	9	15	25	PSYCHOTIC REACTION — Count Five (Hynson-Shirly), Double Shot 104	
6	7	10	14	CHERRY, CHERRY — Neil Diamond (Jeff Barry & Ellie Greenwich), Bang 528	
★7	14	30	40	WALK AWAY RENEE — Left Banke (World United Prod. Inc.), Smash 2041	
8	11	19	23	WHAT BECOMES OF THE BROKENHEARTED — Jimmy Ruffin (William Stevenson), Soul 35022	9
9	10	12	19	I'VE GOT YOU UNDER MY SKIN — Four Seasons (Bob Crewe), Philips 40393	
33	31	24	29	ALMOST PERSUADED — David Houston (Billy Sherrill), Epic 10025	14
34	38	48	58	I CAN MAKE IT WITH YOU — Pozo-Seco Singers (Bob Johnston), Columbia 43784	6
★35	52	88	—	THE GREAT AIRPLANE STRIKE — Paul Revere & the Raiders (Terry Melcher), Columbia 43810	3
★36	51	81	—	THE HAIR ON MY CHINNY CHIN CHIN — Sam the Sham & the Pharaohs (Stan Kesler), MGM 13581	
37	21	11	11	ELEANOR RIGBY — Beatles (George Martin), Capitol 5715	
38	44	61	73	LOVE IS A HURTIN' THING — Lou Rawls (David Axelrod), Capitol 5709	
39	33	35	41	JUST LIKE A WOMAN — Bob Dylan (Bob Johnston), Columbia 43792	
40	34	25	32	SUMMER WIND — Frank Sinatra (Sonny Burke), Reprise 0509	7
41	32	34	45	I CHOSE TO SING THE BLUES — Ray Charles (Tangerine Records), ABC 10840	7
★42	63	80	—	GO AWAY LITTLE GIRL — Happenings (B. T. Puppy 522)	
★43	56	69	90	MR. SPACEMAN — Byrds (Allen Stanton), Columbia 43766	
	57	67	86	COME ON UP	
★67	83	—	—	A SATISFIED MIND — Bobby Hebb (Jerry Ross), Philips 40400	2
68	76	91	—	BUT IT'S ALRIGHT — J. J. Jackson (Lou Futterman), Calla 119	3
69	64	64	82	SAID I WASN'T GONNA TELL NOBODY — Sam & Dave (Prod. by Staff), Stax 198	6
70	70	92	—	DON'T WORRY MOTHER, YOUR SON'S HEART IS PURE — McCoys (Feldman-Goldstein-Gottehrer), Bang 530	
71	68	69	73	I CAN MAKE IT WITH YOU — Jackie DeShannon (Calvin Carter), Imperial 66202	6
72	77	86	89	KNOCK ON WOOD — Eddie Floyd (Prod. by Staff), Stax 194	6
★73	—	—	—	SECRET LOVE — Billy Stewart (Dave & Carter), Chess 1978	1
★74	—	—	—	UP TIGHT — Ramsey Lewis (E. Edwards), Cadet 5547	1
★75	90	—	—	LADY GODIVA — Peter & Gordon (John Burgess), Capitol 5740	2
★76	—	—	—	RAIN ON THE ROOF — Lovin' Spoonful (Erik Jacobsen), Kama Sutra 216	1
77	74	74	84	MELODY FOR AN UNKNOWN GIRL — Unknowns (Bruce Alscher), Parrot 007	4

a truly "complete" sound in every way. Flip is slower, rambles on a bit, but good lead voice."

It was also a recording that emphasised just how innovative those who plied their trade in the Hitsville recording studio could be.

Hitting the piano strings from the underside with a hammer, shaking jars filled with peas to placing a microphone over a floorboard for someone to walk on in order to create a backbeat were all often used, while 'Reach Out I'll Be There' saw the use of a tambourine, minus its ringers and played like a tom-tom. *"We played certain notes through the chord structure"* said Norman Whitfield, *"It caused that eerie sound because we used those suspended notes."*

There was little doubt that Gordy was correct in his assumption that 'Reach Out I'll Be There' was going to be a success and heading for the top, not only Stateside but also in the U.K., with the nondescript local charts also showing it as the top selling single of the day.

It was song that would be covered by the likes of disco queen Gloria Gaynor, fellow Motown artist Diana Ross as well as over one hundred others.

Joe Biden even using it for his 2020 United States presidential election campaign, but none of those covers could capture the vocal brilliance and intensity of Levi Stubbs, coaxed into producing a stand-out performance by Eddie Holland, as the

Tops lead was of the opinion that Holland was wanting him to sing in a higher key, unsuited to his vocal range.

Was the "Just Look Over Your Shoulder", about two thirds of the way through, five words that come completely out of the blue, simply ad-libbed by Stubbs, even although the words can be found in the lyrics if you look on line?

No matter what, 'Reach Out I'll Be There' is one of the all-time classics, but it created something of a problem for the group and Holland-Dozier-Holland, as they had to come up with a strong, chart hitting follow-up.

The Four Tops were now far removed from the relatively unknowns they were a couple of years previously.

When they made that initial trip across the Atlantic in May 1965, Dave Godin and the members of his 'Tamla Motown Appreciation Society' arranged a fan club welcome party, with hundreds of fans turning up, prompting Levi to comment: *"with such devoted fans we're bound to have a nit here one day."*

That hit certainly did materialise and when they landed in Britain this time around, on the back of their No.1 success, if anyone was not aware as to who they were and what they represented, they soon would be as the national press and music magazines were more than eager to run a feature on them.

Not only was 'Reach Out I'll Be There' to be a number one hit in the States and the U.K., it also hit top spot in the Argentinian and Spanish record charts. The former release was as a 33⅓ rpm 7" single, while the latter came in a very collectable picture sleeve.

Heading to the U.K. for the sell-out Saville Theatre concerts, their schedule for their limited time on these shores became tighter by the day.

Friday November 18th saw them booked to appear on the Rediffusion TV 'David Frost Programme' which was preceded the previous evening by an appearance on BBC's 'Top Of The Pops'.

But it wasn't all work and no play, as they found themselves invited to the opening of what was classed as London's No.1 night spot, 'Samantha's', a basement club on New Burlington Street. Not only were them among the opening night celebrities, 'Reach Out' was constantly blasted out over the speakers.

Appearing in the November issue of 'Beat Instrumental' magazine an article entitled - "Meeting The Four Tops" could now be considered obsolete, as the four guys from Detroit were now far from being unknowns and requiring any form of introduction, but for those still off the pace and vaguely unfamiliar with The Four Tops, who the magazine described as looking like *"a gang of footballers, broad shouldered and narrow hips."*

In the interview, Levi spoke of his "adoration" for The Beatles, describing them as "ingenious and brilliant", adding: *"Once they told us they dug our sound and invited us round to their hotel in New York for a few drinks. We were thrilled. Only trouble was we couldn't get through the crowds outside so we had to telephone them."*

He went on to say: *"We only wish people in this troubled world would realise that music is the strongest way to express love at international level. But music is essentially enjoyment. We don't do protest songs and drug songs and all that because we want to entertain the fans and not bring them down, mentally. They've already got their troubles and there's no reason for us to add to them ...."*

The magazine was also quick to add that the Tops music could not be categorised, as they didn't bother to do so such a thing. *"On Stage we tackle everything from country music to out and out blues and we throw in Gospel and comedy for good measure. We sing according to our own mood and according to the mood of the audience."*

Lawrence added to that by saying: *"We don't have to argue about ideas. They simply fall into place. That's what comes from working together for so many years. We just like to keep a big library of songs so that we can switch immediately from entertaining adult audiences to doing what the kids like."*

Speaking in regards to the family atmosphere around Motown, Levi was also quick to mention: *"In our own group, we don't nominate a leader. For instance, I'll be singing lead for a few months more because it seems my voice is angled more strongly for the market. Next it could be Renaldo, or any of the others. We're not kids any more, but we go along with this business of not conforming. We don't stick to the rules."*

The 'New Musical Express' of Friday November 11th also carried something of an introductionary piece – *"Dook, Obi, Grass and Brown flew into town this week, ready to hot up London on Sunday from the stage of the Savill* [sic] *Theatre. Maybe they do sound like an old-time vaudeville act, but in fact this strangely assorted quintet happens to be no less than those very up-to-the-minute stars, The Four Tops."* The article went on to introduce each member in turn, explaining what many would consider their rather strange names.

"These are the handles we've been calling ourselves since we were kids," said Levi. *"The rest of the group started calling me 'Brown' 'cos I used to wear brown a lot when I was younger. But then I figured out the joke, so I started wearing blues an' other colours to*

fox 'em. Good job they didn't end up calling me 'Rainbow'!

"Renaldo's been called Obi since early childhood, but I guess nobody knows why. Maybe people thought a fancy handle like Renaldo was too much to swallow.

"Lawrence? Well, we call him Grass 'cos he's the outdoors-ey type. You bet your life, if ever he can get out an' lounge around in the grass, he will."

Duke wasn't to wait on Levi mentioning him as he butted in with *"I tell you why they call me 'Duke', it was my mother started it. I guess she musta thought I was high class 'cos she used to call me 'Dooky' when I was a little baby."*

Due to the publicity given over to the group and the ultimate success of 'Reach Out I'll Be There', things were reaching fever-pitch by the time the Saville Theatre concert came around and the MC on the night, Tony Hall described the event in his regular 'Record Mirror' column – *"Couldn't write about it last week, because my column has to be at the printers early. But those Four Tops shows at The Saville Theatre the other Sunday were something else!*

"I've never seen a British audience behave in such a traditionally un-British manner. It was simply fantastic!

"The Four Tops were so tremendous that everyone there threw their inhibitions out of the window. It was such a thrill and pleasure to see from the stage a whole theatre full of young people so obviously enjoying themselves. No hysteria. No riots. No tantrums from 12-year-olds. Just plain beautiful, unadulterated enjoyment. In an audience where the sexes were split 50-50. Maybe even more boys than girls.

"It was great to see people get to their feet completely spontaneously and dance where they stood. First, it was the stalls. Then the gallery. Finally, the circle. Everyone, on their feet .... dancing ... waving ... and, especially, singing along with the Tops. It really was a beautiful night.

"There's something about Motown music that alone can evoke such emotion and enjoyment. It's today's sound. Today's spirit. Today's 'feel'.

"Later that night, after the show, Brian Epstein threw a small party at his house in Belgravia. A nice party. With nice people. Like George and Patti. John and Cyn, Mick Jagger, Charlie Watts, Donovan. Georgie Fame, Chris Curtis, Vicki Wickham. Eric Burden, Hylton Valentine . . . people like that. And, of course, The Four Tops.

"The moment the boys arrived; they started dancing. A great scene!

"I spent a lot of time with the Tops that night. They really are terrific guys. They even wanted to take me back to Detroit with them! We talked for hours. About the audience that evening and the effect that the music had on them. We came to the conclusion that music is the one thing that can bring together people of all races, colours and creeds. And that if only young people all over the world could get together and enjoy music the way they did at the Saville that night, no one would ever want to go to war or fight. They'd be much too happy just dancing and singing. And afterwards they'd be completely whacked out and just want to sleep!!! "

Also present on that memorable evening was Penny Valentine who was to share her thoughts in 'Disc and Music Echo'.

"We, the audience, sang at London's Saville Theatre on Sunday night. We sang with the Four Tops from the moment they came on stage with "Baby I Need Your Loving" - because we loved them. Because we knew what it was all about and we wanted to be a part of it.

"The excitement of Sunday was staggering. The theatre was crammed. The audience included Georgie Fame, Eric Burden, Mick Jagger, and Charlie Watts. Raving Mods in tight little sweaters lined the aisles dancing, yelling, clapping.

"Tony Hall introduced the Four Tops to a roar that would not have disgraced a Wembley football crowd. The ceiling lights neatly jumped out of thew sockets and then there they were, grinning, moving, full of their music - the people we had been waiting for so long to see.

"Our hearts were theirs before they stepped on stage. By the time they left, our hands, feet and lungs were theirs too.

"When they heard how we were with them, they made "Baby I Need Your Loving" last for six minutes so we could sing a whole verse and chorus on our own.

"After that they sung only "Michelle" on their own, and even during that quiet rendering their good humour suddenly spilt out and they burst into happy laughter. Then "Shake Me Wake Me.' another six-minute number, with Levi holding the mike out into the stalls and everyone behaving as though it was the Apollo Theatre, New York. "Just Ask The Lonely", 'There's Something About You," a raving "It's Not Unusual." and finally. as we cried and cheered and ran down the aides and danced in our seats and held out our arms to them, 'I'll Be There.'

"Afterwards, when we realised that however long we stood there yelling "More" it wasn't to be, we flopped out, as exhausted as any bunch of artists.

"Backstage in their dressing rooms. the Tops were exhausted and elated. ""Man." they said, "We never expected to see any British audience rave like that. It was too much."

"The rest of the bill naturally had a pretty thin time. The Easybeats were obviously scared of being on the same bill as the Tops for their first British stage appearance, but came off well with funny little jackets and an elf-like lead singer.

"Cliff Bennett is always as competent as expected and gave a relaxed performance to an audience who obviously rated him highly enough to hold them in check before the appearance of the show's stars."

As well as reviewing the show, Penny Valentine added something of a postscript to her article, entitled – "EPHUS! THE 4 TOPS ARE JUST WOLLIPHANT!"

She was to write: *"They are four very jokey gentlemen indeed, the Four Tops.*

"There they were then, Levi Stubbs, Renaldo Benson, Lawrence Payton and Abdul Fakir, absolutely splendidly happy. Everything, they said, was "ephus". And "man", they said "it's really wolliphant in London."

"The Four Tops you see, apart from speaking together and over each other and roaring with laughter and taking the mickey out of themselves, have invented a new sort of language.

"It has been with them now for lost over just over a week. So, it was still novel enough to interject most of the sentences they used, indeed they were delighted with the obvious interest it was causing.

"The whole thing was apparently started by their road manager, Mr. Don Foster.

"We were sitting in the car travelling through Detroit just before coming over" said the Four Tops almost in unison. "We were watching the girls go by, wow! And suddenly Don said "man they sure are ephus". And we turned round and said "Man what IS that all about?" And we found we had a new thing on our hands.

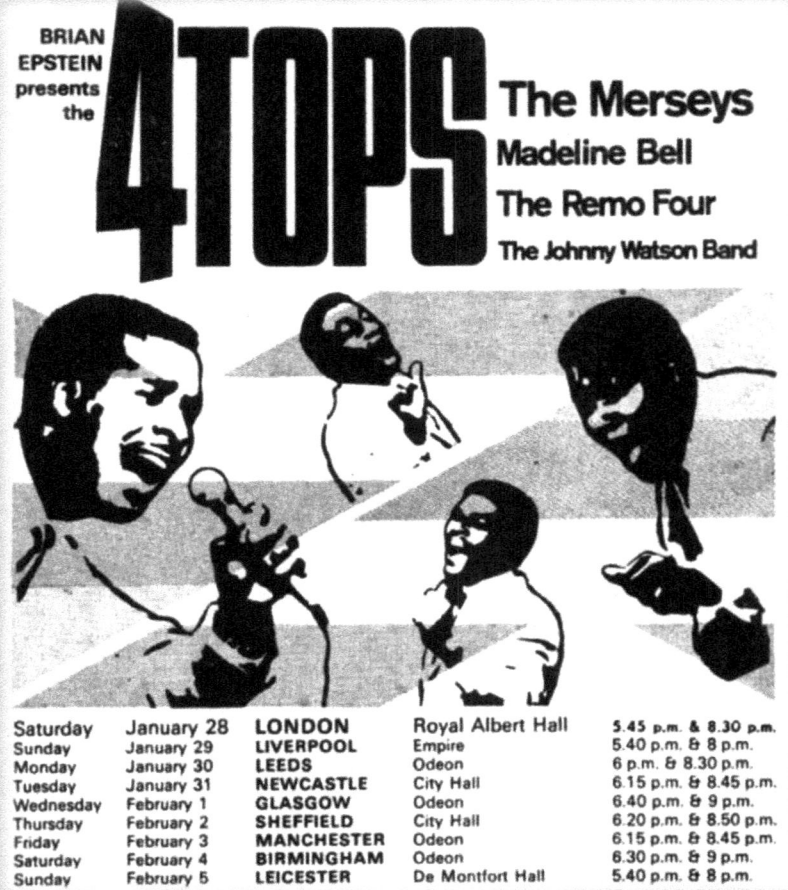

"They got a bit carried away after that and things became mullett and rodent and very spluush. Then they decided they'd gone far enough and their language was complete.

"We record nearly every day. But it's a very free set up. Very wolliphant man, very wolliphant. We go out and play golf with the Miracles and then maybe in the afternoon we'll feel like doing a session so we go into the studio. Or Holland, Dozier and Holland say "Well boys, feel in good voice today?" If we think we'll be better later we don't record during the day.

"We go off and play a quick hand of poker with the Miracles and then 'phone around midnight and say "Sure, we'll have the session now."

"There's no set hours for anything, sometimes we'll be going 24 hours a day but it's real ephus.

"The Four Tops are a very ephus lot of people, a strangely effective combination of their main influences – the Drifters, Four Freshmen and the Miracles. While in Britain, they are planning to buy a Rolls Royce to transport them in glory round Detroit. Ephus!"

A FOUR TOPS DICTIONARY:
Ephus: *Our of sight. The best.*
Wolliphant: *Very good. Okay.*
Mullett: *Average. inclined to be a bit fishy.*
Spluushh: *Terrible*
Rodent: The very lowest and worst.

Twelve hours prior to flying back to the States, the Tops were ushered into the BBC's White City TV Centre to make a recording of their follow up release to 'Reach Out'. It was originally planned to record the group at various location around London, but it was thought that doing the recording in the studio would be a better idea.

The Four Tops were now firmly established on both sides of the Atlantic, although their British fan-

base could be considered as being just a little more enthusiastic their American counterparts. It was now simply a case of maintaining the momentum that had been increasing gradually since the release of 'Baby I Need Your Loving', but was now seeing the foot pushing the acceleration pedal firmly to the floor.

Writing and producing a follow up to 'Reach Out I'll Be There' was certainly not beyond the capabilities of Holland, Dozier and Holland, far from it, and although creating a second master-piece was not impossible, it would certainly test the talented trio. If anything, it was time that was against them, as Berry Gordy insisted that hit followed hit as quickly as possible.

So, October 1966 saw the boy's step into the Golden World studios to lay down the vocals for that follow-up single – '**Standing In The Shadows Of Love**' [its working title was 'My Search Has Ended'] b/w '**Since You've Been Gone**', timed to take the Christmas market, hopefully, by storm, although it was early 1967 before the British public could get their hands on a copy.

The enthusiasm that had heralded the arrival of 'Reach Out' onto the record shelves was not evident upon the arrival of that follow-up. *"Reach Out I'll Be There" was a monster for the Four Tops and this outing "Standing In The Shadows Of Love" is a solid match for that last smash. The driving ode is filled with a solid romance lyric in the quartet's usual powerful style. The sound is that of Motown's finest. "Since You've Been Gone" is another solid side"* was how the reviewer in 'Cashbox' saw it, while 'Melody Maker' was to say: *"The Motown Record Corp. would never miss out on a good thing. The good thing was 'Reach Out I'll Be There', a number one hit in England and America and subsequently the Four Tops follow-up has more than a few overtones very reminiscent of its predecessor. "The churning, kind of skipping beat is there, plus the strings and the urgent vocal, but the record as a whole, doesn't flow quite like 'Reach Out'. Holland and the Doziers [sic] have certainly written* and produced another big hit and it's a nice record despite the lack of new ideas. "The next Four Tops single should be the real test."

Even Duke Fakir was entirely taken in by the side that was to make No.2 in the R&B charts and No.6 on the pop listing in the States and No.6 in the U.K., but for this writer, the 'B' side 'Since You've Been Gone' holds more appeal.

With 'Standing In The Shadows Of Love', or 'Reach Out' part two, or even a re-working of the 1963 Supremes recording 'Standing At The Crossroads Of Love', as some were to dub it, still blasting out of the coffee bar juke boxes, The Four Tops headed back across the Atlantic and with the record heading towards a top ten placing in the record charts, it was announced that due to increased demand for tickets the Royal Albert Hall would host a second show on what was the opening night of the tour - January 28th, the first time in the venues long and illustrious history that a pop package had played two performances. Not only that, a special sound system was fitted for the show – another pop first.

Tony Hall, who had compared the Saville Theatre concerts, and who had originally been unavailable for this tour somehow managed to wangle an escape route and compared five of the nine shows, the others having former Migil-Five drummer/vocalist Mike Felix as MC.

It seemed like only yesterday that the Hitsville tour had played to barely half-filled theatre's and now here was the UK music press telling their readers that the Tops would be flying into London from Detroit on January 26th at 7.10am on Pan American PA 56 and forecasting that they would be receiving a welcome reception comparable to only what The Beatles could expect.

Promoted once again by Brian Epstein, the tour dates, following the 14,000 sell-out shows at the Albert Hall, took in the Liverpool Empire on January 29th; Leeds Odeon on January 30th; Newcastle City Hall on January 31st; Glasgow Odeon on February 1st; Sheffield City Hall on February 2nd; Manchester Odeon on February 3rd; Birmingham Odeon on February 4th and Leicester de Montford Hall on February 5th. If that wasn't enough, the day after that final performance in Leicester, they were to head for the Questor Theatre in Ealing where they would be filming a thirty-minute special for BBC2 in front of a specially selected audience.

A week-long series of television appearances were then scheduled in Italy, Germany, France and Spain.

With the demand for tickets having forced that second show at the Royal Albert Hall, there is perhaps little need to say that the concerts were a success. For those who were foolish enough to miss out, or required a nudge to catch one of the other shows around the country, the columnists in the music press told their readers what they had missed, or what they could expect.

"Not even in the wildest moments of our wildest dreams could any of us have imagined what happened on Saturday night at London's Albert Hall at the second appearance in Britain of The Four Tops" wrote Penny Valentine in 'Disc and Music Echo'.

"It was the Saville Theatre twenty times over. It was spectacle on a scale you wouldn't have expected outside a mammoth film production.

"It was fanatical exultation of the Nuremburg Rallies, the incredible enthusiasm of a World Cup football crowd.

"And it was there for the Four Tops before they even set foot on the stage. They said afterwards that all they had to do was to go out there. Everything was waiting for them. They didn't have to work for it.

"But they did work for it. They sang because of it and because this was final proof, if it were needed, of the tremendous love relationship the Four Tops have with their audience, and their audience with the Four Tops.

"The Tops ran on stage to a cheer which soared to the roof and bounced back off the lights. In the stalls, they rushed forward and surged fifteen deep round the base of the stage.

"Behind the stage they stood and swayed and clapped their hands above their heads and cried. Where I was, they sat on each other's shoulders, danced in their seats and sang "Reach Out", "Wake Me Shake Me" [sic], "Baby I Need

- 40 -

Your Loving" – even "Climb Every Mountain".

"Thirty-five Tamla Minutes Of Joy" was headline following the show in Sheffield. "Those Four Tops knock spots off the rest of the pops. And after catching their 35-minute act at Sheffield's Civic Hall last Thursday I can see how the Tamla Motown foursome earned their name.

"There's nothing new about their routine – feet shuffling, finger clicking and arm waving dates back to 50's – but for sheer artistry, they stand out a mile.

"Lead singer Levi Stubbs burst into "Baby I Need Your Loving" and it was a signal for communal singing. "Hand clapping, foot stamping and whistling followed as the Four Tops swayed, danced and sang their way through 'Just Ask The Lonely', 'The Same Old Song' and 'I Can't Help Myself' and 'Climb Every Mountain' (a golden lesson in harmony).

"Their smash hits 'Reach Out I'll Be There' and 'Standing In The

Shadows Of Love' brought a barrage of sweets from the audience, how those fun loving guys lapped it up."

There have been hundreds of women associated with Motown over the years. There is one, however, who surfaced in 1967 and remains a mystery and whose true real identity is unlikely ever to be revealed. Her name was Bernadette. The track, although giving the credits to Holland-Dozier-Holland, is basically the work of Lamont Dozier who was to say in later years that it was inspired by a beautiful Italian girl he knew at school as an eleven-year-old, basically his first love.

Duke Fakir was to add to the mystique surrounding her. *"Nobody knows who she is, except for three or four people. Even Berry doesn't know. He asked that at Levi's funeral – "I have to find out who this Bernadette is" and she was there."*

Just like in 'Reach Out I'll Be There' with Levi's "just look over your shoulder", 'Bernadette' catches you completely off guard with the plaintiff cry of "Bernadette" as the record moves towards its final grooves.

"It's the greatest number we have ever done" they said *"It's another fantastic song by Holland-Dozier-Holland, and this time it's even better than 'Reach Out'"*, Fakir was to say and perhaps it would have been a much better choice of a follow up to their No.1 hit, something echoed by 'Billboard' in its review of the new release in March 1967 – **Bernadette** b/w **I Got A Feeling** – *"Hard-driving rocker will quickly surpass their successful "Standing in the Shadows of Love" at the top of the Hot 100. Outstanding performance by the group is right in the Motown bag."*

In 'Home of The Blues' magazine, the forerunner to 'Blues and Soul', its review in issue No.9 of April 1967, which also featured the group on the front cover, due to them having been voted the readers favourite group, the review read – *"Less commercial than their more recent recordings but certainly as good. Lacks the impact and sameness of their last. Levi sings extremely well. The song? Not very tuneful. Another good flip – but from their album."*

Backed by The Andantes and The Originals, there was another voice behind the microphone when the recording was laid down on January 1967, with Eddie Kendricks of The Temptations stepping in to supply the tenor part, as Duke was un-well on the day of the recording.

The track, however, didn't quite surpass 'Standing In The Shadows Of Love' on the Stateside R&B chart as it only reached No.3, although it did fractionally better on the pop charts, reaching No.4.

In the U.K., where it stalled at No.8, the 'New Musical Express' shouted – *"What a sensational sound! What an invigorating and thoroughly irresistible Rhythm! What spine-tingling excitement! This is undoubtedly one of the most thrilling groups on disc today, and here we have the celebrated Motown sound at its peak of perfection.*

"The song itself is constructed in much the same style as their last two hits though of course the tune is slightly different. I rate it as better than their last one, but not quite as good as 'Reach Out'. Obviously, a hit!

"Flip: More of a swinging, hand-clapping beat here, emphasised by rattling tambourine and clanking piano. Type of song we associate with the Supremes."

Peter Jones of 'Disc and Music Echo' was equally enthusiastic – *"A tremendous performance again that big swelling and big selling sound, highlighting a son that may be just a shade short on commercial melody."*

In between the chart topping 'Reach Out I'll Be There' and hot on the heels of 'Bernadette', there were two album releases – 'The Four Tops Live' and 'On Broadway'.

Stateside, there had been countless 'live' albums released on the Tamla label from as early as 1963, featuring the likes of Mary Wells, Little Stevie Wonder, The

Miracles, Marvin Gaye, The Marvelettes, The Supremes, a various artists one recorded live at the Apollo and another on a similar vein, recorded live in Paris. None of the latter two mentioned were to feature The Four Tops. On this side of the pond, prior to the release of **'The Four Tops Live!'** in February 1967, however, there was only the Stevie Wonder issue, The Supremes 'At The Copa', the March 1964 issue of 'Various Artists – On Stage' and in May 1965 The Motortown Revue which was to see the tracks taken from the previously mentioned artists live albums that had been released in the States and 'Live In Paris'.

Recorded at The Roostertail, 100 Marquette Drive, Detroit, in August 1966, the album was what at the time was a typical Tops concert, mixing their hits with standards such as 'If I Had A Hammer' and 'The Girl For Ipanema'. It even includes a version of The Supremes hit 'You Can't Hurry Love'.

Album sleeve notes were written by the compare on the night, disc jockey Scott Regen, who actually sings, or perhaps that is better versed as adds his voice to 'Reach Out I'll Be There'. Regen had also featured as the subject matter behind the Edwin Starr Ric Tic recording 'Scott's On Swingers' released in 1966.

In the review that appeared in 'Home of The Blues', the reviewer, whilst confirming that the group are *"the most popular of the Detroit acts"*, he or she adds that on the album they *"sing well enough, but somehow there is not too much atmosphere......I do not feel that the standards included in the album are necessary for any collector of Motown music, although it proves how talented the group are."*

'Billboard' reported another live recording in their issue of September 23rd 1967, with Eliot Tiegel reporting under a heading – "Room at the Top, Four Tops Find In Customizing Songs for Clubs",

"Los Angeles -The Four Tops, who closed their first booking at the Cocoanut Grove with a live LP recording, have learned to custom-tailor their repertoire to suit the level of the room. Four years ago, the Detroit quartet was still hustling around the "chitlin' circuit." Today, the male vocalists are a top Motown act and a new find for such rooms as the Grove and New York's Copa, Washington, D.C.'s Shoreham, Cherry Hill, N.J.'s Latin Casino and Hollywood Miami's Diplomat - all forthcoming bookings.

"On recordings, the quartet sings the pop love songs of Eddie Holland -Brian Holland and Lamont Dozier. On stage, they dip into the Broadway and film repertoire for adult - oriented tunes which fit their pleasant harmonies.

""We try to keep the composer's beauty in the material," explains Renaldo Benson, who along with Levi Stubbs Jr. Lawrence Payton and Abdul (Duke) Fakir, formed the group 13 years ago.

"During their Grove engagement the quartet included an Academy Award medley as its customizing for the film-oriented audience. Wade Marcus, the group's musical director, and Payton produced the live LP, for which Motown's chief engineer was flown here.

"Benson, the "philosopher" in the group. feels that as a result of the Grove appearance, the group sought a wider musical scope. "For the last four years we've been playing rock concerts where sound is not really that important. Here, we had to truly work to stimulate the audience." Benson says they never "jive an audience" because they've been through the scuffling bit and appreciate the opportunity to work in the big time.

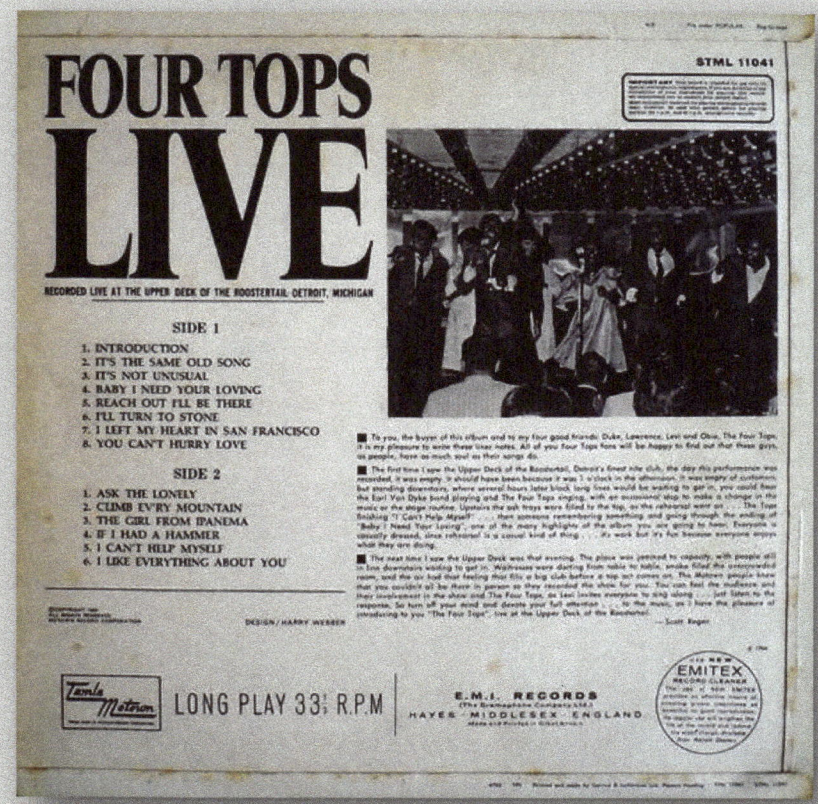

- 43 -

"The Tops' troupe numbers nine (including rhythm section) which involves a healthy weekly nut, but they are earning substantially more than their "chitlin' circuit" salaries of from $1,000-$1,500.

"Two months ago, the artists worked the Whisky A Go Go on the Sunset Strip, where their repertoire was more tuned to their Motown single hits. Their booking into the downtown prestige room so soon after this exposure was a surprising bit of scheduling.

"When they play colleges, students ask for the single hits.

This fall the quartet is planning a new act for the Ivy circuit, which pays considerably better than the "chitlin" clubs.

"The Tops now plan to begin producing records, which is a characteristic of the Motown operation where executives are artists, and writers are artists."

Cashing in on the fact that The Four Tops were now Motown's top act, Gordy delved into the archives and pulled out recordings that were, all but one, made back in 1963 and put them together for the 'On Broadway' album, released only in America. It was an album that Levi was to say was his particular favourite.

Despite the live album arguably having only limited appeal, but considered by the group to reaching a peak in their long road to success, it still managed to hit the number one spot in the R&B chart. 'On Broadway' would presumably have even less appeal to the masses, as despite showing the versatility of the quartet, it was, as it said on the label, simply Broadway standards, with its No. 15 R&B placing and 79 on the pop charts justifying that it was a Gordy gamble that just didn't pay off.

"This is a complete change of pace for the usually hard driving rockers from Detroit. They invade the Broadway scene and come up with a sure-fire hit LP.

"Smooth performances abound, with 'Maria' from 'West Side Story'. 'What Did I Have That I Don't Have' and 'Mame' standouts" read the 'Billboard' review, while 'Cashbox' was to say: *"The Four Tops deliver a package of R&B flavoured Broadway tunes. They create a great deal of excitement as they perform, and the album is likely to prove a real mover with the artists' legion of followers."*

No matter what, while the 'Live' album gave those unable to see the Tops in concert a sense of "being there", neither On Broadway, or the 'Live' album caused as much as a ripple in The Four Tops tidal wave of popularity and it was soon to be a case of normal service is resumed in May 1967 with '**7 Rooms**

Of Gloom' b/w '**I'll Turn To Stone**'

Recorded in January 1967, but not released until just over three months later, it was to give the Tops their first doubled sided hit in the States, despite the initial reviews in the music press simply saying *"No information available on the flip side at this time."*

Upon its release, '7-Rooms of Gloom' was considered simply an addition to their long list of hits and one that "could go all the way".

The British musical press was somewhat divided. The 'Record Mirror' – *"Song about the lonely house without the girl – the backing is effectively separated from the vocal which is compulsive and driving but maybe not as raucous as their last couple of discs. A hit quality shines through and although this isn't quite as commercial as their last, it is certainly better. Flip is a more conventional Tamla beater with all the ingredients. Top Fifty Tip."*

'The New Musical Express' - *"GEE whiz, what a wildie from the Four Tops. Faster in pace, and different in concept, from anything they've attempted before. Starts relatively slowly, with an imploring semi-shouted plea from Levi - then suddenly the whole thing erupts with the fury of a volcano. Storms along at a fantastic pace, with Levi maintaining a despairing heart-cry, while the other boys chant the main melody line on echo.*

"It's framed in a busy Tamla scoring, heightened by emphatic double-time tambourine. The whole effect is quite shattering!

"Flip: Reverts to the familiar Motown bouncy-jerk beat. Levi solos the verses, with ensemble treatment of the chorus.

"Both sides are Holland-Dozier-Holland compositions, of course. Tipped for the charts."

Released in the States in May 1967 and in Britain a month later, the record was to hit No.10 R&B and No.14 Pop on the 'Billboard' charts, whilst also failing to hit the top ten in the U.K.

In regards to that Holland-Dozier-Holland-Taylor penned 'B' side, it was to see Berry Gordy begin legal proceedings as he attempted to sue Tony McCauley and Mike D'Abo composers of The Foundations hit 'Build Me Up Buttercup', as it was considered to be a carbon copy of 'I'll Turn To Stone'.

With the release of that record by

The Foundations, along with the publicity of the legal action, not to mention the continues plays on the Northern Soul scene, 'I'll Turn To Stone' was to resurface as an 'A' side, something that it was worthy of in the first place, in September 1972.

Controversy was to rear its head once again in 1974, when Abba's No.1 hit 'Waterloo' was also to bring comparisons to that same song.

'7-Rooms Of Gloom', like the previous releases – 'Reach Out I'll Be There', 'Standing In The Shadows Of Love' and 'Bernadette' was included in the groups fifth album '**Reach Out**', as was 'I'll Turn To Stone', released in July 1967.

Akin to The Four Tops previous albums, except of course the 'Second' one, it was something of a mismatch of tracks. A dozen in total and taking out the previously mentioned ones, the remaining seven consisted of 'I'm A Believer' and 'The Last Train To Clarksville' – both hits for The Monkees, Tim Hardin's 'If I Were A Carpenter', The Left Banke's 'Walk Away Rennee', 'Cherish', previously recorded by The Association and from the Motown stable of writers 'Wonderful Baby' and 'What Else

Is There To Do (But Think About You).

Reviewed in the 'Record Mirror' as *"Long awaited hit album from the Tops, with four fine 'A' sides and their versions of some of the best non - R & B tunes around - try their "Walk Away Renee" which'll surprise Left Banke fans, or their version of the Neil Diamond-penned Monkee million seller "I'm A Believer"'* It was considered worthy of four stars.

The 'Billboard' reviewer, however, was of the opinion that *"This is the distillation of the Motown sound, polished to a gleam and delivered with a full measure of commercial soul. The Tops are among the smoothest performers in the business and they are really tops with 'Standing In The Shadows Of Love' and 'I'm A Believer'."*

Allowing the album to meander up and down the charts, reaching No.3 R&B/No.12 Pop in the States and No.4 in the U.K, Motown released what would be the groups final single of 1967, with '**You Keep Running Away**' b/w '**If You Don't Want My Love**' hitting the shops in August.

That recording, given four stars in 'Blues and Soul', although if taking in John Abbey's comments, it could well have received less – *"Definitely getting into a rut are Motown's top male attraction. This latest effort is rather ordinary material. Tuneless and mid-pace – even Levi can't do much with it"*, was, however, to be the penultimate single release, for the time being at least, to materialise from the group's partnership with the dynamic trio of Holland-Dozier-Holland.

It was certainly a vast distance from the trio's best Four Tops offering, considering what had gone before, but in-house problems relating to obtaining what was in their opinion a fair return for their Motown input, Eddie and Brian Holland and Lamont Dozier decided that the time had come for the parting of the ways and in 1968 walked out the door.

Due to their Motown contract still having two years to run, they were unable to work, or write, for another label, but this 'gardening leave' did not see them sit idle, as they spent the time setting up their own labels – Invictus and Hot Wax, although it has been long suggested that such plans were in place prior to their conflict with Motown.

Had The Four Tops Motown contract been up for renewal at this particular time, it is worthwhile considering if they would have followed H-D-H out the door and joined the new label. Hearing Levi and the boys belt out the likes of 'Give Me Just A Little More Time', 'Everything's Tuesday' and the rest of Chairmen of the Board's Invictus output captivates the imagination.

Obviously, General Johnson had such a distinctive voice which was emphasised on all the Chairmen of the Board records, but wouldn't you like to hear their No.1 smash hit sung by Levi?

"That was like having your best girl leave you" Duke was to say of the departure of the multi-talented trio from Motown. *"We kept saying, "Y'all are gonna leave?! What are you gonna leave for?" They said, "We just can't get along with Berry..." You gotta be kidding!" We were devastated. We couldn't find anyone to produce us. Smokey produced a thing or two. Norman Whitfield, he was too busy with the Temps. He said: "I wouldn't know how to even begin with you all." We couldn't find a producer, so we recorded some songs that were just ok."*

With the disruption caused from the in-house rumblings, Motown therefore decided to return to the 'Reach Out' album for the groups next two singles – '**Walk Away**

Renee' b/w 'Your Love Is Wonderful' followed by 'If I Were A Carpenter' b/w 'Wonderful Baby'.

Of the former, one reviewer wrote: *"Their revival of the beautiful Left Banke hit must be a far bigger smash that their "You Keep Running Away". Although the poignancy of the original is lost, the strong melody and emotional lyric suit the Tops, and the usual danceable beat is here. For once, though, the cluttered Tamla back-drop doesn't help things along. A simpler approach with the accent on the lead vocal would have been better. Flip just doesn't even sound like the Tops but it's a swinging sound anyway. Top fifty tip."*

Of the latter release, it was: *"Delicate instrumental opening to this revival of the Tim Hardin penned Bobby Darin hit. Levi Stubbs injects this with his usual sobbing soulful quality and it's different enough from the other versions to garner after Walk Away Renee revival. Flip is a big - sounding Tamla item with potent backing."*

In regards to 'Walk Away Renee', released first in the U.K., hoping to capture sales in the Christmas marketplace, it rose to No.4 in the charts and was quickly pushed out in America where it failed to scale similar heights, having to be content with a top twenty, rather than a top ten placing. 'If I Were A Carpenter' did likewise, although it was to peak at No.7 in the U.K.

When asked why they had released 'If I Were A Carpenter' from an LP, as their current single, Lawrence Payton replied: *"We travel around so much, we have to leave decisions like this to others."* Adding, perhaps not wanting to rock the boat; *"But it is a good number and I'm sure it will do well for us. We don't get the time we would like to record singles. Besides in the States it is mostly LPs now anyway."*

It had been a long journey from 'Baby I Need Your Loving' through to the present day, their versatility putting them on a pedestal above their Motown stablemates, but had they reached a crossroads in their career. A crossroads where the signpost had been removed?? To say that Motown was on a heading on a downward spiral would be incorrect, but the hand-clapping, foot-stomping, dance-floor filling records of only a few months and years previously, the theme tunes of countless lives, had more or less come to an abrupt halt.

Messrs Holland and Dozier were of course not responsible for every one of those memorable tunes, but they proved to be the inspiration to the others who attempted to match their creditable output.

So, at the crossroads and in limbo, Berry Gordy certainly could not afford to lose his prize recording assets, even if he did not consider them as such, but the quartet were not prepared to rest on their laurels, drift along aimlessly, dining out on their past hits and achievements, both at home and abroad, the latter being arguably more appreciative, but the ambition and determination to achieve more was still burning strong within their hearts and minds.

Berry Gordy's focus was being distracted elsewhere, the Holland brothers and Lamont Dozier had left for what would be pastures new but The Four Tops could still hold an audience on the palm of their hands, mainly due to the voice of Levi Stubbs, despite the overall unity between the quartet -

"*His raw power and emotional bursts lend themselves to the group's propensity toward broken heart -sad "baby I need you" type of songs. His compatriots blend nicely in supporting roles but have weak voices individually. Collectively, they are fine.*" wrote a reviewer following an August 1967 concert at the Cocoanut Grove in Los Angeles.

If the Four Tops fan base didn't quite take to 'If I Was A Carpenter', 'Walk Away Renee' receiving considerable plays in some of the more conservative night clubs, then the release of '**Yesterday's Dreams**' b/w '**For Once In My Life**', went down like the proverbial lead balloon.

"*Love the Four Tops in their pulsating, primitive state*" wrote the reviewer in the 'Daily Mirror' of August 8th 1968, "*but this one has slipped into low gear. Not for the charts.*"

Penny Valentine was perhaps not quite as scathing in her review of the record in 'Disc and Music Echo' nine days later. Under the bold heading of 'Can The Four Tops Keep Their Fans? She penned: "*I like this record, but more than that I will be very interested to see what happens to it, and people's reactions.*

"*It is a very different Four Tops from which we have been used to. No raving. In fact Levi Stubbs sounds positively strait-jacketed into submission. He sings with great restraint on this gentle song with a girl backing group and not a sign of the Tops around.*"

"*DJ Johnnie Walker said it reminded him of "Go Now" and I was cross because I wanted to be the first to point it out. Yah. Anyway, it does -tremendously so.*

"*It was produced with warmth by Tamla's lady* [sic] *producer Ivy Hunter, and has a nice round sound. I'd like to see it do well, but I fear Four Tops fans are going to miss all the straining and emotion we've had in the past.*"

But it was back to the doom and gloom from whoever did the reviews for 'Melody Maker' – "*Not a Holland-Dozier or even a Holland song, and the Tops suffer accordingly.*

"*This is a Hunter-Bullock-Goga-Sawyer composition – would you believe? Hunter's bit weren't bad, but Bullock's...Grim days ahead for the Tops, one feels.*"

Following on the coat tails of the single came the '**Yesterday's Dreams**' album, released in the States in August 1968, and it was more than strange to see a Four Tops album with the names Holland-Dozier-Holland appearing beside only one of the tracks.

It is a complete mismatch of material, from the title song to covers of Bobby Hebb's 'Sunny' and The Monkees 'Daydream Believer' – yes again, there is little to excite even the staunchest Four Tops fan, with the exception of the Ashford/Simpson penned 'Can't Seem To Get You Out Of My Mind' perhaps coming closest to what you would expect from the quartet.

Considering that duo's eventual Motown output, in particular with Marvin Gaye and Tammi Terrell, it is surprising that Gordy did not allow them to work hand in hand with the Tops in order to see if a strong, firm and positive working relationship could be established. But it wasn't to be.

What the powers at be, sitting in the ivory towers on West Grand Boulevard were thinking in regards to The Four Tops around this time is anyone's guess, but whatever it was, it was far from positive.

With the imminent departure of the company's star writers and producers, Gordy certainly had a lot on his plate, but more attention should have been paid to the goose that laid the golden egg.

In something of a belated attempt to re-capture some of that old magic, it was decided, somewhere along the line, to dive into the dusty basement vault and see what was there. They didn't look very far, or perhaps didn't look at all, simply releasing 'I'm In A Different World' a track that had been recorded in late 1967 and squeezed out of that 'Yesterday's Dreams' album!

It was down to Penny Valentine in 'Disc and Music Echo' to get down to the nitty gritty with her review of '**I'm In A Different World**' b/w '**Remember When**', also taken off the 'Yesterday's Dreams' album. She wrote, under the heading 'The Four Tops Hit You In

The Stomach': *"For some unknown reason I feel guilty about raving over, the Four Top's records. I want to stand up and shout hurray, hurray and leave it at that, but I feel everyone will immediately say smugly, "Oh well, she's biased, she ALWAYS likes Four Tops records"* (not in fact true - I was dubious about "Yesterday's Dreams").

"The question is should I care what you think? The answer is NO. So, hurray hurray anyway!

"And now to the record. Well, they've gone back to Holland, Dozier and Holland and the production is probably the best to come from Tamla for ages.

"The actual melody is hard to find on first play because the song breaks up a lot in a solid jellified way. But play it more - and it's worth every minute of needle wear - and you'll find exactly why it hits you in the stomach - pow!

"There is one expert key change, and that Tamla bass player is in there again playing as only he can. Some superb strings on the chorus and a gem of crisp cymbal playing make it a joy to listen to, dance to and love. And the words, the words! Oh my."

That in effect was that. The partnership between The Four Tops and Holland-Dozier-Holand had come to an end, fizzled out like a damp firework on November 5th.

Concert bookings continued to fill the diary, but visits to the recording studio were few and far between, although 1969 began with one of those rare excursions to Hitsville to set down the vocals for the Bristol/McNeil composition **'What Is A Man'** b/w **'Don't Bring Back Memories'**.

Although having not quite drifted into obscurity or fell with the also-rans, it was something of a surprise to see the 'New Music Express' proclaim – "Tops Rocket Back", with 'What Is A Man' included

amongst the music papers "chart tips" for the week of May 24th 1969.

"I imagine that 1969 will go down in pop history as "the year of Tamla." At the moment, everything that appears on this label seems to have a head start on all other releases - this, coupled with the Four Tops' established popularity, is sure to send them rocketing back up to the Chart.

"A bit different from their previous disc, in that it's mainly a group vocal - and a very catchy tune too.

"But the familiar Tamla trappings are unmistakeable – heavily accentuated beat, tambourine, swirling strings and biting brass. The Tops, plus the flowing and colourful arrangements, makes this extremely easy on the ear."

Reviewer, Derek Johnson could claim to be only partially correct, as the record barely limped into the top twenty in the U.K., managing No.16, while failing to make the top fifty in the States.

'What Is A Man' was also, somewhat predicably, on the album 'Four Tops Now!', released in the summer of 1969 in the States, but held back until September in the U.K.

By now, The Temptations had ventured onto Cloud Nine and Motown was on the verge of change, and not for the better it could be argued.

In a 'Record Mirror' article entitled 'Motown Magic?' it examines a handful of album releases, including **The Four Tops Now**', with the following – *"The Four Tops Now" shows the boys'* progression from the thumping teen-oriented chart numbers to more sophisticated material, and although this is obviously a question of hobson's choice, due to the absence of Messrs Holland-Dozier-Holland, it has made the Tops fit themselves into another bag.

"Their bouncily emotional version of 'Little Green Apples' contrasts with an impassioned 'Eleanor Rigby' - neither to my taste, but their beautiful 'What Is A Man' matches up to an orchestral and ambitious 'MacArthur Park' - both superb. They do 'Fool On The Hill' without too much histrionics, and the other tracks are all beautifully recorded and performed. They are: 'The Key', 'My Past Just Crossed My Future', 'Don't Let Him Take Your Love From Me', 'Do What You Gotta Do', 'Don't Bring Back Memories', 'Wish I Didn't Love You So' and 'Opportunity Knocks'."

Was it worth spending thirty-seven shillings and five pence on? The record reviewer in the 'Daily Mirror' certainly though so. "There can be no quartet in the world to compare with the Four Tops and this album, which must rate as their best ever, is a great tribute to their sheer professionalism."

With such mediocre material and Motown seemingly concentrating on the more progressive sounds of The Temptations and resting on the laurels of Marvin Gaye's 'I Heard It Through The Grapevine', Levi and the boys could be considered the forgotten men of Motown, perhaps

more so, when the company directive simply scoured that 'Now' album for their quartets next single release opting for the Jim Webb composition **'Do What You Gotta Do'** b/w **'Can't Seem To Get You Outa My Mind'**.

Somewhat strangely, or perhaps the flagging sales across the States, were behind the decision to only release this one only in the U.K., Ireland and certain European countries, along with South Africa, Australia and New Zealand forcing the serious collectors amongst the fanbase to buy around a dozen copies of the record due to the variety of picture sleeves and pressings. But that decision to avoid the U.S. market paid dividends

as the track, produced by Frank Wilson, Lawrence Payton, Wade Marcus brought positive reviews – *"considerably less in tempo than their earlier 'I'll Be There', it is every bit as potent. I'd like to see the Four Tops high in the charts with their new one. Very nice ballad appealing sung by the Tops."*

"The Four Tops have chosen a very different sound from their last single 'What Is A Man', which deserved success and never got it. 'Do What You Gotta Do' is a Jim Webb song and is taken from the group's new album. It is a pleasant enough sound without the quality of the old hits."

It was to breach the U.K. top twenty at No.11.

October 1969 saw a columnist in the 'New Musical Express' ask the question: *"Remember those Four Top heydays when 'Reach Out I'll Be There' scorched to No. 1 and many of us sang and swung to their music at that fantastic concert they gave at the Royal Albert Hall?"* before going to say, what everyone was more than aware of: *"Things have been a little quieter of late, but record buyers who've put the Tops 'Do What You Gotta Do' at No.17 in the NME Chart may like to know that the group's reputation could hot up considerably again, if plans for a*

Motown package tour materialise in the near future."

In that same respected weekly publication, a couple of months later a more absorbing article written by Alan Smith was to appear – *"Complaints that the Four Tops have been releasing old LP tracks as singles – 'Do What You Gotta Do' was a case in point - were answered by Top Levi Stubbs in person when we* talked on a London - Detroit phone line at the weekend.

"The trouble," said Levi, "is that the original material we've had to consider recently just hasn't been that fantastic. We've been trying to get something different together. man. Somethln' with some guts in it somethln' real earthy.

"We've been happy with what we've done in the past, sure. But the time has come for the Tops to keep pace with what's happening in music, We wanna do somethin' wild, somethin' free. We've started to dress casual too.

"Anyway, we hope to be there in England next spring and we're determined the Tops will have a coupla dynamite singles coming out soon."

Having thumbed their nose at the fickle American market those who sat around the boardroom table at the Motown headquarters were to suddenly turn their backs on the more than supportive U.K. market and gave a Stateside, European, South African and Australian release to '**Don't Let Him Take Your Love From Me**' b/w '**The Key**'. Both tracks taken off the 'Four Tops Now' album.

Although both tracks were passable, producing a minor hit, Motown were clearly scrapping the bottom of the barrel when it came to the groups output, something that continued to be obviously with the release of the '**Soul Spin**' album as 1969 edged to a close.

One track on this album, the Pam Sawyer/Beatrice Verdi composition 'Lost In a Pool Of Red' is considered to be the closest the Tops came to heading down the same route taken by The Temptations with their 'Cloud Nine'.

With the Holland-Dozier-Holland trio now nothing more than ghostly footsteps on the floorboards at West Grand Boulevard, the production side of the Four Tops recordings was handed over to Frank Wilson, who had overseen the 'On Broadway' album, with Paul Riser, Henry Cosby, Gene Page and Wade Marcus taking on the arrangements.

It mattered little who sat behind the controls, as 'Soul Spin' was once again little more than a mixture of one side of compositions from the Motown stable composed by the likes of Messrs Sawyer, Cleveland, Hinton, Verdi, Robinson, Gorman, Hunter and Goga, tracks that were never going to be hits in a million years, with the rest of the album being nothing more than covers – the likes of 'Got To Get You Into My Life', a Lennon/McCartney composition and a U.K. hit for Cliff Bennett, 'The Look Of Love', recorded by Dusty Springfield and composed by Bacharach and David, and The Mamas and Papas hit 'California Dreamin''.

Back to that 'New Musical Express' article mentioned a few lines back which concluded: "*In the States, however, the group seems to have reached a special position where they're accepted as top-line artists and that's that. This is why a great deal of the ballyhoo about the group had now died down to be replaced by a quiet respect for its talent.*"

A NEW DECADE AND A NEW BEGINNING

The Autumn of 1968 had seen Berry Gordy move from Detroit to Los Angeles, while the following year Motown began to move bit by bit from the now deteriorating surroundings of Detroit to the Californian sunshine.

Infatuated by Diana Ross and determined to make Motown a force in the movie industry, he had taken his eye off the goose that had laid the golden egg, but as 1968 came to a close, Gordy had a wide smile on his face as he had the top three records in the R&B top fifty – Marvin Gaye's 'I Heard It Through The Grapevine', The Temptations 'Cloud Nine' and Stevie Wonder's one time Four Tops 'B' side 'For Once In My Life'. There were also three Motown albums in top five of the album charts, while the Billboard 'Hot 100' saw Motown again claim the top three placings. The Marvin Gaye and Stevie Wonder's sides joined by Dian Ross and The Supremes with 'Love Child'.

"All this without Holland, Dozier and Holland" Gordy was to exclaim.

Then along came the Jackson Five, pushing any interest in The Four Tops well and truly onto the bottom shelf.

The sixties had seen The Four Tops arrive on the music scene in a blaze of glory, amassing hit after hit, captivating audiences across the world with their harmonious voices and tight stage act, but by the end of the decade, they had stagnated beyond belief due to the poor handling and inadequate recording material put their way by Motown, with the group certainly paying the price for what was Motown's transitional period.

The group readily admitted that 'Do What You Gotta Do' was a bad track – was the 'B' side stronger? But it was a question of who was more frustrated, the group for the somewhat substandard material that Motown was issuing with 'The Four Tops' emblazoned on the label, or their fans, brought up on a diet of classic, unforgettable tunes. Motown needed a wake-up call and the new decade was to be a time for change, in more ways than one.

Suddenly, there was a change for the better. Out of the blue, the Tops suddenly found themselves back on track, their star once again high in the sky and shining brightly.

Early spring 1970 saw, for some unknown reason other than to remind people that The Four Tops were still in existence, or perhaps in an attempt to boost record sales on the back of something of an impromptu visit to the U.K. for a number of television appearances, Motown re-issued '**I Can't Help Myself**' b/w '**Baby I Need Your Lovin'**', which was also to see releases across Europe and surprisingly, it was to reach No.10 in the U.K. charts.

The arrival in Britain was to also co-incide with the groups plans for an International Union for Harmony, an initiative planned to help young and old alike who were less fortunate than others.

Speaking to the press in regards to the re-issue of 'I Can't Help Myself', Levi was to comment: *"I really can't understand why they didn't put 'Barbara's Boy', which has been released in Europe, out here too, but then I'm sure they have*

good reasons and I won't argue with that. We can always find something fresh from a number when we go back to it, and I'm sure though that 'I Can't Help Myself is going to be good for us."

When questioned in regards to the changes around Motown with the departure of Holland, Dozier and Holland, he was diplomatic answering: "I like all types of music and we don't want to get hung up on one bag, but with Holland - Dozier - Holland it was like a marriage. But the people still think of us as the rock-it sock-it group, so I guess the punch is still there. In our cabaret act we include many Broadway show tunes, we don't just stick to our regular material because there are so many other beautiful tunes."

In regards to the previously mentioned 'Barbara's Boy' - a Hinton/Sawyer track from the 'Soul Spin' album, the 'Holland' section of 'Cash Box', which related to the country, not one of the brothers, saw a Pete Felleman write: "When I flew in The Tops for the annual Grand Gala Du Disque last February, I swore we'd get a hit out of the event and it worked. Since then, Belgium, France, the German block and the Scandinavian zone have released 'Barbara's Boy', which curiously enough is not available on single in either the U.S. or the U.K."

The U.K. trip of March 1970, however, was one that Levi Stubbs would have wanted to put well and truly behind him, as he was to find himself in the news for all the wrong reasons.

"Pop Star Bailed On Drug Charge", "Pop Star Goes For Trial", "Four Top Singer In Drug Case" shouted the headlines, with the articles that followed all telling the same story - "Levi Stubbs, 33, lead singer of the American pop group, the Four Tops, was remanded today at Bow Street court, London, until Tuesday, charged with unlawful possession of cocaine and 12 rounds of ammunition at the Mayfair Hotel, London, last Thursday'

"Stubbs was allowed £1,000 bail - £500 in his own recognisance and £500 surety provided by the group's manager, Ralph Garcia. The singer wore a dark pin-striped suit for the court appearance, which lasted three minutes."

Returning to court just over a week later, Levi was cleared of the drugs charge, but was fined £25 for possessing the live ammunition.

"AMERICAN SINGER CLEARED OF DRUGS CHARGE. Levi Stubbs (33) lead singer with the Four Tops American pop group was acquitted by an Inner London Sessions jury yesterday of unlawfully possessing cocaine at the Mayfair Hotel London in March.

"Mr Colin Hart-Leverton prosecuting had alleged that two tubes containing cocaine worth between £200 and £300 were found in a jacket belonging to Stubbs when police went to the hotel after a "tip off". Stubbs had said in evidence he had no idea who could have put the drugs in his jacket.

"Mr Ralph Garcia, their business manager, said yesterday he had never known Stubbs to take drugs.

"Autograph hunters and people claiming to be friends were continually knocking at the door and the group always invited them in.

"When the police were searching, he went to his own room with police and found a man there whom he did not know and who had apparently got in through a communicating door.

"The jury took fifty-four minutes to reach a verdict of not guilty. Earlier in the absence of the jury Stubbs had pleaded guilty to possessing twelve rounds of live ammunition. He was fined £25. Mr Montague Waters for Stubbs said the ammunition had been in Stubbs' holdall for a very considerable time and he had not remembered that he had brought it with him.

"Mr Stubbs said at his London hotel last night that he was very happy about the outcome of the case and he thought British justice was excellent. He said that Britain had one the fairest legal systems in the world. Here a person was innocent until proved guilty in America it was the other way around."

It certainly was the other way around, as Britain held The Four Tops close to their hearts, while their homeland tended to treat them indifferently, like some one-time chart toppers, now seeing out the last days of their careers on some nostalgia circuit of shows. Then suddenly, and totally unexpected, came both a single and an album release in the space of more or less days.

The single release, as in the recent past, was nothing original, but a cover of a 1958 hit for Tommy

Edwards '**It's All In The Game**' b/w '**Love Is The Answer**'. Somewhat strangely, the stunningly performed tune was to give the guys their first chart success Stateside, in three years, reaching No.24 in the pop charts and No.6 in the R&B charts. Released in the U.K. a couple of months later, it was to hit the No.5 spot in the charts.

and Billie Rae Calvin of The Undisputed Truth on backing vocals, was an obvious choice to see further release as a single and like the album, it was to see chart success, a No.4 R&B hit and No.11 in the pop charts, compared with the album's respective No.3 and No.21. When released in Britain it climbed as high as No.10.

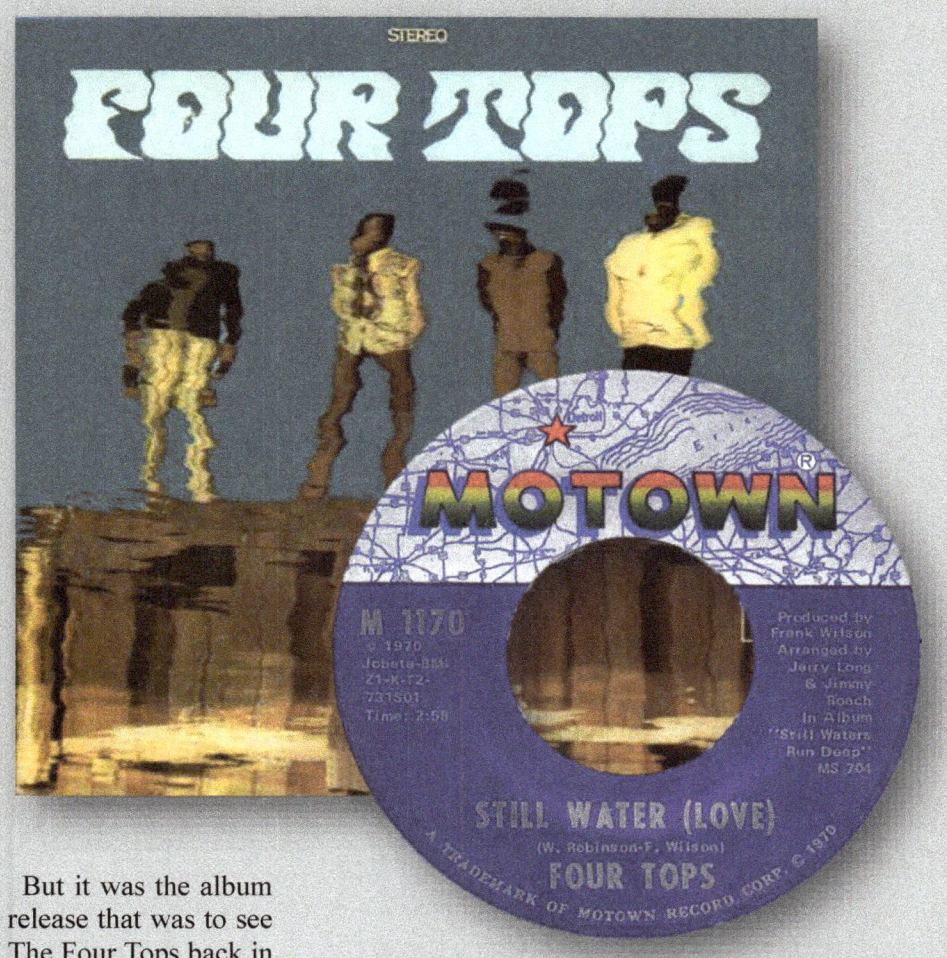

But it was the album release that was to see The Four Tops back in the spotlight and back where they belong, with '**Still Waters Run Deep**'.

As in the past, that album would contain the unnecessary 'fillers' such as 'The Elusive Butterfly' and 'Everybody's Talkin'', but it would also receive countless plaudits and it was considered to be one that would bring the group much overdue success.

The title track, composed by Smokey Robinson and Frank Wilson, with Brenda Joyce Evans

"'*Still Water*' was a great song," said Duke Fakir. "*It was a lifesaver; it pulled us out of a hole. That was probably the last significant thing we did at Motown. We recorded another album, but it was just ok.*"

The shadows of Brian and Eddie Holland and Lamont Dozier continued to hover over Motown and in particular The Four Tops, but in an interview with 'Beat Instrumental, Levi Stubbs was to have his say.

"See, we started with Motown back in 1963. We had the Holland, Dozier and Holland songs for us right from the start, so the relationship got to be like a marriage that sure wasn't heading for the divorce courts.

"We had a rock-it-to-'em, sock-it-to-'em reputation and those writers kept us going just fine. But you can't blame the guys for wanting to do their own thing.

"Me, I like all kinds of music. Maybe, when things are settled, it'll be a good thing, because we can do different things, and anyway we're giving opportunities to be heard to about fifty other writers.

"We figure that you should never lose a chance if there is an idea there. If one of us comes up with an idea, we will troop right off to the studios. It could be 4.00am or whatever. What comes first with us is our music.

"But when you lose the writers you depend on, you have to make changes. We're into the college circuit thing now, rather than cabaret. Don't ask me why it is, it is just that the audiences seem that much more real. But we don't have to change the material.

"We do a lot of show-tunes, for instance, as well as original material from guys like Norman Whitfield and Frank Wilson. But there's a limit to how often you can keep coming up with the old hits, so you can say that we're very much in an experimental stage.

"The thing is that Tamla is getting so big that it can stand losing guys like Holland, Dozier and Holland, but we felt it more than most of the others. What I'd say is that there is a change running right through the company. Put it down to experience, I guess, but the guys there just aren't relying on the old formulas.'

"It is now that much more subtle. Not so much of the sock-it-to-'em, at all levels through the company. I guess some of it is based on the old concept, but a whole lot more is happening that you really have to listen to closely otherwise, you miss out on where it's at.

"We've been working for a couple of years now to get just the right material. We know we have to change. You can say that albums are more important right now, but once you've been up there at the top of the Hot Fifty... well, it's something you don't get out of your system.

"The future? `Sure there's an argument that it's wrong to keep bringing out album tracks as singles. But if you just don't have the same fantastic service from the writers, as we did with Holland, Dozier and Holland, then you've got a problem. `Like I was saying, losing them was like ending a marriage, but who knows what could happen in the future?"

Under the direction of Frank Wilson, the group were to admit that it was a totally different environment than it had been under Lamont Dozier and the Holland brothers. Speaking in Goldmine' in 2002, Duke Fakir was to say: *"Frank Wilson spent a lot more time in the studio, experimented with the tracks a lot more, changing rhythms, backgrounds.... He might create four or five versions of the same track. We worked much harder with Frank, but it was a joy, because all the while we were creating."*

Back in the public eye on the recording front, they had never been out of it when it came to live performances, then as 1970 moved to a close, Motown attempted something different, pairing the Tops with the now Diana Ross-less Supremes, a pairing that would see the release of the album '**The Magnificent Seven 7**'.

Produced by the well-established, husband and wife team of Nickolas Ashford and Valerie Simpson, along with Clay McMurray and Duke Browner.

The twelve track album was something of an unusual mix, with the likes of the Ashford/Simpson Marvin Gaye and Tammi Terrell hit 'Ain't Nothing Like the Real Thing', Diana Ross's first post-Supremes hit 'Reach Out And Touch', which was also another Ashford/Simpson collaboration, Sly and the Family Stone's 'Everyday People', the Tops own 'Without The One You Love', 'A Taste Of Honey', a track The Beatles had recorded for their initial album and the Ike and Tina Turner monster hit 'River Deep – Mountain High'.

That latter track, along with 'Reach Out And Touch', 'A Taste Of Honey' and 'Everybody's Talking' were also to appear in a 7" format. Six of the tracks were also issued on a 7" 33⅓rpm juke box format in the States.

American fans were treated to the album '**Changing Times**' in September 1970 [it appeared in the U.K. the following year], yet another mixture of tracks that the quartet handled with the normal ease and professionalism.

Despite the obvious 'hit you between the eyes' stand-out track, the 'Billboard' reviewer was found to be quite positive.

"*The consistent Four Tops have an interesting and winning pressing here. "The pairing of 'The Long And Winding Road' and the title song surround the selections which include such fine numbers as 'Try To Remember', 'Raindrops Keep Falling on My Head', 'Something's Tearing at the Edges of Time' and 'I Almost Had Her (But She Got Away)' are among the other top cuts with that Four Tops stamp.*"

Somewhat surprisingly, there was no glowing reference for 'Just Seven Numbers' which was later to appear as a single.

The following year, 1971, was to see two further album releases pairing up with The Supremes in '**The Return Of The Magnificent Seven**' followed by '**Dynamite**'. The only track of any real significance to come out of those albums was the leading one on the former – "You Gotta Have Love In

Your Heart', although Motown was to release '**I'll Try Not To Cry**' b/w '**One More Bridge To Cross**' from the 'Return' album and '**Impossible**' b/w '**If I Could Build My Whole World Around You**' from 'Dynamite'.

On the singles front the next release was the late 1970 recording of the Pam Sawyer/Gloria Jones (under the name LaVerne Ware) penned '**Just Seven Numbers (Can Straighten Out My Life)**' b/w '**I Wish I Were Your Mirror**'.

A reviewer in 'Cash Box' was of the opinion that the 'A' side was "*Moving back into the style the bears the Four Tops trademark, with a pulsating ballad from the 'Changing Times' LP*". Their suggestion that it would "carry the quartet high in the top forty sweepstakes" however, was to prove marginally out, as it was to only hit No.40 in the pop chart, although it did make No. on the R&B one. It was to just break into the U.K. top 40 at No.36.

It was then back to the collaborations with The Supremes for the next attack on the singles market, but '**You Gotta Have Love In Your Heart**' b/w '**I'm Glad About It**', both tracks extracted from that 'Return Of The Magnificent Seven' album and it was never going to breach the higher reaches of the charts, making

only to made a minor impression in the U.K., hitting the No.25 spot, while on the other side of the Atlantic, you have to scour the top 200 to find it tucked away at No.154. "*An embarrassment for us all*" uttered Mary Wilson.

Strangely, the 'Cash Box' reviewer was to pen the following - "*The electrifying combination that made the "Magnificent Seven" is about to return with an album previewed by this delightful rock outing. Side has the power of a cleanly produced dance track and some outstanding vocal fireworks to assure monster receptions.*"

If such a release was an embarrassment to the artists, then it would surely have served as something of a wake-up call to the label, but The Supremes, without Diana Ross were as far down the pecking line as the Tops, when it came to first class material, as Motown continued to stagger down a road of uncertainty.

In America, and away from the collaborations with The Supremes, and from a solo perspective, the only other issue by the group from 1971 was to be the aptly named '**In These Changing Times**' b/w '**Right Before My Eyes**', released in May, another two nondescript sides that do little more than take up a line or two in their lengthy discography.

The decision to release this particular track was clearly proved wrong by it failing to make higher than No.70 on the pop charts.

A couple of months later, the autumn of 1971 was to see something of a first, a U.K. recorded release – '**Simple Game**' b/w '**You Stole My Love**'.

During their U.K. tour of the previous year, they were approached by Tony Clarke, producer of the Moody Blues, with a track entitled 'Simple Game', written by the groups keyboardist Mike Pender and released by them as a 'B' side.

Impressed by what they heard, the Tops were persuaded to make their way to the Wessex Studios in Highbury, north London, the following day, where they laid down the vocals, backed by members of the Moody Blues and Blue Mink, over the backing track that had already been recorded by Pinder and Moddy Blues guitarist Justin Hayward.

Hayward was later to recall: "*Berry Gordy liked 'Simple Game,' that was the plain truth of it. He came over to meet with Tony Clarke, our producer, and then Tony was assigned The Four Tops, which was like a dream for all of us.*

"*The rest was done by an arranger called Arthur Greenslade, an English arranger, best known for his work with 'Son of a Preacher Man' singer Dusty Springfield. He translated the rock songs to suit the Four Tops, but British musicians did the playing.*

"*I certainly played on them, and I*

loved every moment of it, and just being in their company and the fun and the laughs.

"They were kind of grown up as well. They were a few years older than us."

There were two further tracks to materialise from that 'Simple Game' session - 'You Stole My Love,' another Clarke/Hayward composition, with the former working under the alias of Gurron, when the song was issued as the B-side to 'Simple Game'. The other was Pinder's 'So Deep Within You'. Hayward was to add *"it was probably only myself and Mike that played on those records."*

'Simple Game' was to soar to No.3 in the U.K. charts, giving the group their biggest chart success since' Reach Out I'll Be There', which seemed like a lifetime ago.

It wasn't until January 1972 that it was to see a release in the States, 'Billboard' considering it a *"Powerhouse rhythm number with a potent lyric line has it to put the group way up the Hot 100 and soul charts topping their "MacArthur Park" in short order. Could go all the way."*

'Cash Box' were equally positive: *"Totally fresh approach for Levi Stubbs and crew which should prove to be their biggest success in many chartings. Moody Blues material gets one hell of a reading."*

It didn't, however, quite live up to those reviews, as it only managed to nudge its way into the R&B top forty at No.34.

Another autumn of 1971 release, although not in the U.K. and mentioned a few lines back, was **'MacArthur Park (Part 1)** b/w **'Part 2'**.

A huge favourite of Duke Fakir's, who was to say in an interview: *"I would think our music would continue to go where it is with things like 'McArthur Park', but I don't think we'll go too far into other things, we want to keep it so that we can sing any type of music, and keep a selection. Psychedelics would basically not be quite our thing."*

He was to continue: *"The group handle many of their intricate vocal arrangements themselves, notably on 'McArthur Park', which has done well for them as an American single. Lawrence Payton did the vocal arrangements and Gil Askin [sic], the Supremes conductor handled the instrumental."*

'In Those Changing Times' was perhaps more than an apt production for The Four Tops to cut and they drifted into another vein with the album '**Nature Planned It**', released in the spring of 1972, which once again showed their versatility, something that had always shone through since their early days on the scene.

These changing times were also evident away from the recording studio and the record charts, as the one-time youth club/discotheque floor fillers of the Holland - Dozier - Holland era, although they were still popular, mainly on the U.K. northern soul scene, were to be edged to the side across the Atlantic, with an article in 'Billboard' magazine mentioning that those Frank Wilson produced records were finding favour in the clubs.

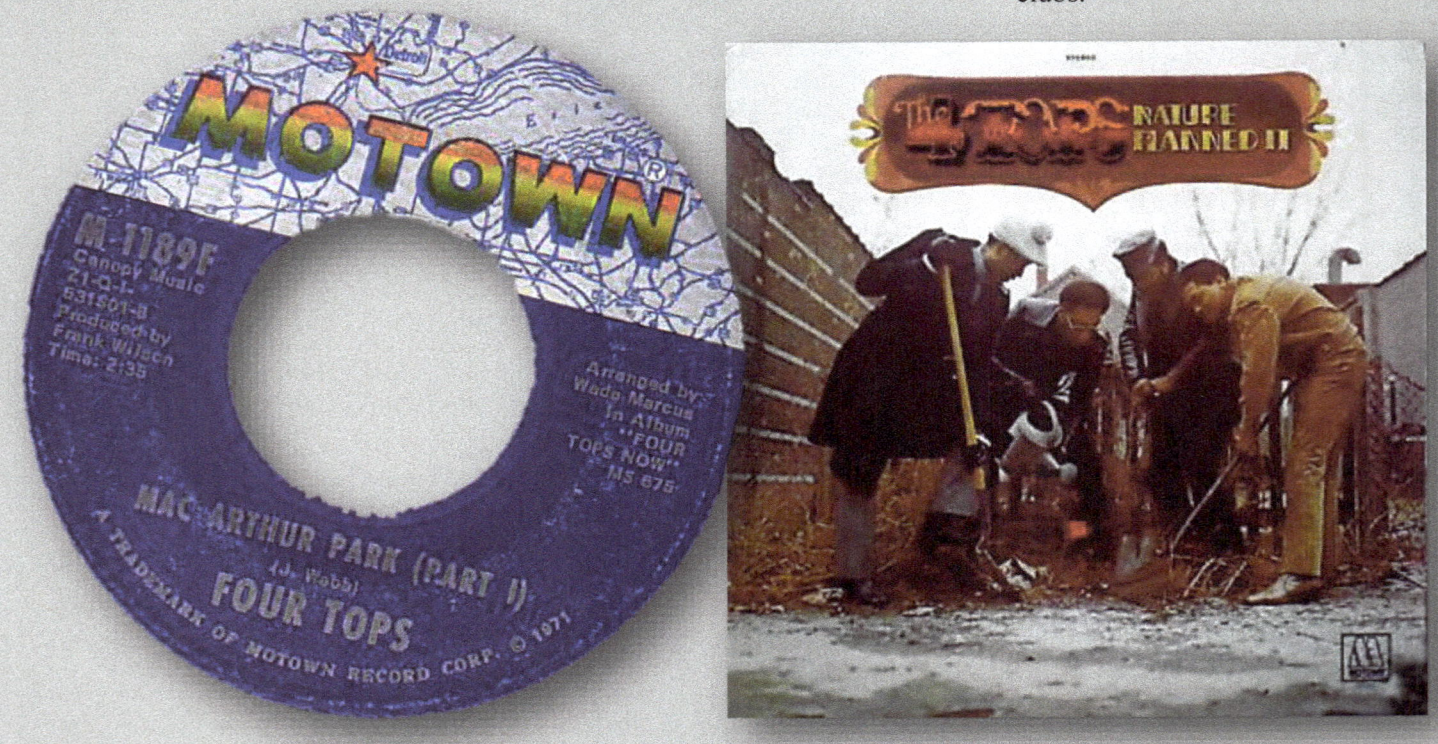

"Steppers are a growing culture of African-Americans, aged thirty-five to fifty-five, mostly from the Chicago area, who like to dance in a style similar to swing dance.

"According to Chicago disc jockey Joe Ferguson, who hosts the largest dance sets in the Windy City, the favourite Four Tops songs with Steppers are 'Still Water', 'That's The Way Nature Planned it' and 'It's All In The Game'.

"These songs fill up the dance floor. Steppers are galvanised by the beat."

A far cry from 'Something About You' and 'I'll Turn To Stone'!

As the clocks struck midnight on December 31st 1971, no-one, certainly not Levi Stubbs, Duke Fakir, Obe Benson and Lawrence Payton, was aware as to what the following twelve months would conjure up.

Recording wise, it would be something of a strange year as there was a distinctive mix between American and U.K. releases.

On the latter front, February had seen the re-lease of '**Bernadette**' b/w '**It's The Same Old Song**', followed in May by yet another duo release with The Supremes – '**Without The One You Love**' b/w '**Let's Make Love Now**'. The 'A' being more than familiar from the Tops early days.

A couple of months later, '**Walk With Me**' b/w '**L.A. (My Town)**' was to hit the shelves and then in November, Motown, once again lacking in any constructive ideas, decided to release yet another Four Tops/Supremes recording – '**Reach out And Touch**' b/w '**Where Would I Be Without You Baby**'.

Stateside there was '**I Can't Quit Your Love**' b/w '**Happy Is A Bumpy Road**' released in April and '**(It's The Way) Nature Planned It**' b/w '**I'll Never Change**' in August. Both

recordings taken from the 'Nature Planned It' album and they would both see a U.K. release the following year.

Throughout their career, The Four Tops never had a 'leader'. Yes, Levi was more often than not the front man on stage, while as time passed, Duke tended to be more to the fore as the group's spokesman, but there was never one of the foursome looking to 'outdo' the others. They were a group, lifelong friends, The Four Musketeers, one for all and all for one. However, 1971 was to see one of the quartet thrust into the spotlight, not on stage behind a microphone, but due to his prowess whilst sitting at home with a notebook and pen.

It was May 15th 1969 and The Four Tops tour bus was on the road, passing in the vicinity of a number of anti-war demonstrators at Berkeley's Peoples's Park. What was initially a peaceful protest got completely out of hand, ending in multiple injuries and a fatality amid claims of unnecessary police brutality and violence.

Having witnessed such harrowing scenes, Obie Benson wondered as to what was behind it all and upon returning to Detroit put his thoughts down on paper and along with Al Cleveland set out the lyrics to the song 'What's Going On'.

Initially, Benson suggested that the Tops should record it, but they were of the opinion that it was a 'protest song' and not something they wanted linked with and despite all Benson's attempts at trying to convince the others that it was in fact a song of love and understanding, his three amigos dug their heels in and turned it down.

Playing a round of golf with Marvin Gaye, Obie told him about the song and offered it to him to record. Back at Gaye's house, following the golf course outing, Benson played the song on a guitar, but Gaye felt that it would be better suited to another Motown act, The Originals.

Benson persisted with the suggestion that Gaye should record it and after he had made a few suggestions, one or two additions to the melody and lyrics, Gaye finally agreed to go into the studio and record it.

'What's Going On' was to become one of Motown's most memorable records with the album of the same name going on to be a permanent fixture in the 'Billboard' chart for over a year, hitting No.1.

Somewhat strangely, Berry Gordy was quoted as saying that the record was the worst he had ever heard.

With Motown having decided to shift the major part of its operation out to California, the Tops had not been instantly dismissive of the idea in regards to re-locating and took a trip across country to see what was what, but then, having given it all the once over, they said thanks but no thanks.

"When we left Motown, we had to leave because there were too many artists at one time," said Levi Stubbs. "When you have Stevie Wonder, The Supremes, The Jackson Five, The Four Tops, The Temptations, Marvin Gaye, Smokey Robinson and the Miracles, Martha and the Vandellas, The Velvelettes, aw, shucks, Shorty Long, Jnr. Walker, you've got all these people. What record company could you think of with a roster like that, and I'm not even through.

"They had so many hit artists until it was virtually impossible to service them all."

"We didn't feel we were getting the attention at Motown, so we just moved on" Lawrence Payton was to add."

There was also another side to the story, as Duke Fakir was to relate.

"It was very difficult. At that time, we weren't sure what was really going on. We had that album [Still Water] that really pulled us out, but after that we couldn't really get into a groove. It's like the promotion wasn't great. We kept wondering.

"Wait a minute. What's going on here? Can we live without Motown? We started thinking as men. Is this big umbrella keeping us alive? What would happen if we had to leave? Could we do it on our own? Could we go out there and do something?

"The contract was expiring as they were planning to move to the West Coast. Berry was concerned about getting to L. A. and getting stuff done.

"Ewart Abner [Motown's vice-president] was not a big fan of the Four Tops. We went in to negotiate our new contract. There were a couple of things that we were going to change; a few more guarantees. He looked at us and said, "Nah, can't do that. In fact, y'all had your run. I really think y'all are through."

"We said, "what?" He said, "I think y'all are through." I said, "So, you're not going to do any of these things we're asking for in the contract?" He said "Nah, I'm not interested." We left."

It is more than certain, that once out of the confines of Abner's office, a few choice words were said and who could have blamed the boys, but despite the success they had brought to Motown over the years, they accepted the news in the same professional manner that they recorded those memorable records and approached their shows at the numerous venues across the world.

Duke continued: *"We started talking about it and said, "Well, I guess it's time to find out who it is. We talked to one of the promotion men who was a good friend of ours. We said, "Do you know anyone out there who is interested in the Four Tops? We just got out of contract. We're looking for a deal. He was on the west coast a lot.*

"Two days later, he came back and said, "Man, look what I got". He had a piano version of 'Ain't No Woman (Like The One I've Got)' and 'Keeper Of The Castle'.

"I said, "Damn, these are some great songs. "Where did they come from?". He said, "Two writers at ABC/Dunhill. They would love to have you.

"I said, talk to the guys and have them call me. Let's see if we can make a deal.

"Jay Lasker [one of the founders of Dunhill Records] *called me and said, "Come on out here. I think we can make a deal." They flew us out and we sat down and made a great deal.*

"We ran into these writers [Dennis Lambert and Brian Potter] *and they played these two songs, which were good enough for us to sign, because they were hits. I said, "Man, this is great stuff. It ain't Holland-Dozier-Holland, but they're still good songs.*

"It was hard to leave, but we were ready to find out. We were really anxious to find out if we could do this, plus we were hurt."

Strangely, Abner had acted off his own back, no discussions around the boardroom table with any of the other Motown hierarchy, nothing.

The ink was barely dry on those Dunhill contracts when Duke was to receive a telephone call from Berry Gordy.

"Duke, why didn't you call me when Ewart wouldn't pick up the contract?" Gordy asked.

"Well, that's your president" came the reply.

"Duke, you should've called me" responded Gordy. *"I never would've let you guys go. If ever y'all want to come back, anytime, y'all got it."*

Gordy's surprise at one of his prize assets jumping ship must have stung and perhaps saw him sit down and made him realise that their departure was in part down to him having taken his eye off the ball with the group. Allowing what was arguably second-class material being issued under their name and not paying enough attention to the needs of his artists.

In hindsight, it was a move that The Four Tops should have made sooner, perhaps heading out the door of Hitsville at the same time as Lamont Dozier and the Holland brothers, but loyalty was a word that was entrenched in The Four Tops make up, written through them like words in a stick of rock. Thankfully, however, their, let's say, prolonged stay at Motown did nothing, or at least little, to affect their reputation when it came to selling theatre tickets. They could still pull in a crowd no matter what corner of the world they were to find themselves in.

With Understandably Great Pride

ABC/Dunhill Records Proudly Welcomes To Our Family

The Four Tops

STARTING OVER

September 1972 saw ABC/Dunhill announce the signing of the group and taking everything into consideration, it could well have been a gamble for both sides.

In regards to the group, many would have been of the opinion that they were living on past laurels when it came to their recording output, despite the fact that they could still fill theatres and night clubs around the world, so were Dunhill signing four guys whose best days were considered behind them?

Placing the record company and the group together could also be considered as something of a gamble, as here was a company who had arguably no experience in working with a Soul or R&B artist or artists. The nearest they had touched was Thelma Houston with her Jim Webb collaboration 'Sunshower' in 1969, with much of their past output having centred around the likes of Steppenwolf, Three Dog Night and The Mamas and The Papas, but this was not seen as anything of a hindrance by either the group or Dunhill. If anything, it was the exact opposite.

"We heard through company sources the Four Tops might be coming to us" said Dennis Lambert, one of the writers seconded to the group upon their arrival at their new label, "and since we have always been fans, we started working on a few songs aimed at them.

"The group has always relied on the song as a vehicle for their success, primarily using the Holland-Dozier-Holland team who were the greatest exponents of marrying a song to an artist."

While the company as a whole, had little experience with anyone like the Four Tops, Lambert on the other hand, had previously worked with Mary Wells and Jerry Butler. His co-writer, Brian Potter had co-penned the first Small Faces hit 'Whatcha Gonna Do About It' and their 'One Tin Soldier', so there was experience on both sides of the recording studio.

The new boys settled in quickly and Messrs Potter and Lambert got their heads together and came up with '**Keeper Of The Castle**' b/w '**Jubilee With Soul**', released in October 1972.

Four Tops To ABC/Dunhill

HOLLYWOOD — Jay Lasker, president of ABC/Dunhill Records, has announced the signing of the Four Tops to the label. The group, formerly on Motown Records, has been one of the top recording and nightclub acts for a number of years.

The Four Tops are Levi Stubbs, Renaldo Benson, Abdul Fakir and Lawrence Payton. They signed with Motown in 1965 and their first record, "Baby I Need Your Loving," was a hit and was followed by their recording of "I Can't Help Myself." Their solid success has been further registered by such hits as "Reach Out" and "Bernadette."

New LP In Works

The Four Tops are currently working on their first album for ABC/Dunhill and are being produced by Steve Barri with Dennis Lambert and Brian Potter. The group wrote half the songs in the LP. The new association supports the creative freedom long-sought by the Four Tops. States Abdul Fakir (Duke) for the group, "We are tremendously pleased that our new alliance will allow us to expand creatively with freedom of material and direction and with the back-up of concentrated promotion and publicity." The group has been singing together for 15 years.

Pictured here are the Four Tops surrounding their producers (center l. to r.) Brian Potter, Dennis Lambert and Steve Barri. The Four Tops are: (l. to r.) Abdul Fakir (Duke), Renaldo Benson (Obie), Levi Stubbs and Lawrence Payton.

"*It may seem a bit unusual at first to see The Four Tops with new label affiliates. But the talent that has made the group one of the most successful in the pop/r&b field is still ever present. Culled from their "Keeper Of The Castle" LP, comes this title tune with renewed vigor, and excitement certain to put the Tops right back on top*" was the opinion of the reviewer of the single in 'Cashbox' with the record giving the quartet their first Top Ten hit since 'Bernadette' some six years previously. It had been that long!

Released on the Probe label in the U.K., it was to peak at No.18 in the charts.

An album of the same title saw release the following month and was also to receive critical acclaim – "*The message-filled title track, penned by producers Dennis Lambert and Brian Potter serves as the spotlight of the group's first album for the label. 'Love Music,' 'Ain't No Woman (Like the One I've Got)' and 'Remember What I Told You To Forget' are among the other 11 powerful tunes. With Levi Stubbs Jr. upfront on most cuts the sound and material is tops.*" – 'Billboard'. While 'Cashbox' was to say: "*The quartet's first for the label should quickly put them back into the brightest spot-light of soul and pop acceptance. On both ballad and up tracks, they've never sounded better. Title tune is their latest single, a success which could be followed by release of many of the other tracks including 'Ain't No Woman,' 'Turn On The Light Of Your Love' and particularly 'Remember What I Told You To Forget'. Produced by Steve Barri, Dennis Lambert and Brian Potter, these twelve tracks will keep the group spinning on the charts for a long, long time.*"

Speaking in regards to the single and album Lambert was to say: "*After the signing, we talked to the group at great length about what they wanted to do and say, which is when we came up with 'Keeper,' as a concept for the LP. The song was meant to represent something philosophical, but it's still a pop song and nothing is going to make it anything else.*"

When asked what they had done to make it a rapid return to the charts for the group, Lambert continued: "*It's hard to pinpoint anything specifically different. One thing we did was help gather some of the songs they had written and let them record them, which was a somewhat new experience for them. We worked with them in building their abilities as writers.*

"*We also let the group become totally involved with the vocal arrangements, hoping to give them something to my rather than making them victims of the chorus.*"

Co-producer Potter was to add: "*At one time, there was a definite Four Tops trademark, a sort of grinding, chugging beat in four - four time. 'Standing in the Shadows of Love' was this kind of song, and we tried to get away from this.*"

Perhaps aiming something of a dig at Messrs Holland-Dozier-Holland, whilst at the same time also attempting to add further credibility to his and Potter's work, Lambert threw the following into the mix: "*Many writers feel if you have a hit, you can do the same thing sideways and upside down and have three more hits.*

"*We think this is a certain road to disaster. We try to stay as far away from a song we've been successful with as possible. This is why 'Ain't No Women' is more traditionally soul than 'Keeper'. I think that through most of the Motown years, the group was thought of as a great lead singer with three guys yelling in the background,*"

Potter was to add. "*But they are really a consummate vocal group. This is why we have three of them singing lead at various points and all singing together on many cuts.*" Lambert agreed. "*Levi is a fine singer and we tried to put songs back into realistic non-screaming keys for them and move them away from their formula sound. And we wanted to avoid the monotony of the one guy doing all the singing.*"

So, the seeds were sown on what was the third phase of The Four Tops career. It had been a long journey from those now distant days of The Four Aims, scrimping and scraping, making a few dollars here and there, if they got paid at all that is, to the international stardom of the present day.

Whilst the quartet would always be more than eternally grateful to Berry Gordy, Lamont Dozier and the Holland brothers, they had now turned a corner. They were with a different record company and a look at the credits on their 'Keeper Of The Castle' album you will find the names Fakir, Stubbs and Benson amongst the composers, their input now being much more than simply supplying the vocals.

Speaking after the successful release of the album, Obie Benson was to say: "*It's all fantastic and we're very happy with Dunhill. They have captured a new feeling for us, one that we have never experienced at all before.*"

Although there had been little to celebrate chart wise in the U.K., that 'Keeper Of The Castle' album received numerous plaudits on British shores. Take the review in the 'Acton Gazette' on Thursday January 11th 1973 – "*It's a good job not everyone makes albums like the Four Tops. or we'd all be queueing outside the record shops every morning waiting to get in. For polished professionalism and harmony. there are very few to touch them which is why they are still one of the biggest names to come out of the Tamla Motown stable. If you shut your eyes and listen hard, you can almost see them bouncing through their formation dance routine, under the masterful direction of vocalist supreme. Levi Stubbs.*

"*The title track is already a hit, but the rest of the songs are just as impressive, possessing a subtle blend of the traditional Tops chorus lines and magical orchestral arrangements and a wilder wah-wah backing, which has become so popular recently.*

"*It's an album of rare brilliance and a must for all lovers of that sweet soul music.*"

Having hit the ground running with 'Keeper Of The Castle', equally important was finding the right follow-up, as no-one wanted to be classed as 'one-hit-wonders' within the confines of Dunhill Records and beyond.

When that follow-up was released in January 1973, some might have doubted the wisdom of Dunhill going with the second track on the 'Keeper Of The Castle' album – **'Ain't No Woman (Like The One I've Got)'** b/w **The Good Lord Knows**', both Potter/Lambert compositions, but those doubters were proved wrong as it secured the Tops a bigger hit than 'Keeper', hitting No.2 R&B and No.15 on the 'Billboard' Pop listing, doing even better on the 'Cashbox' charts

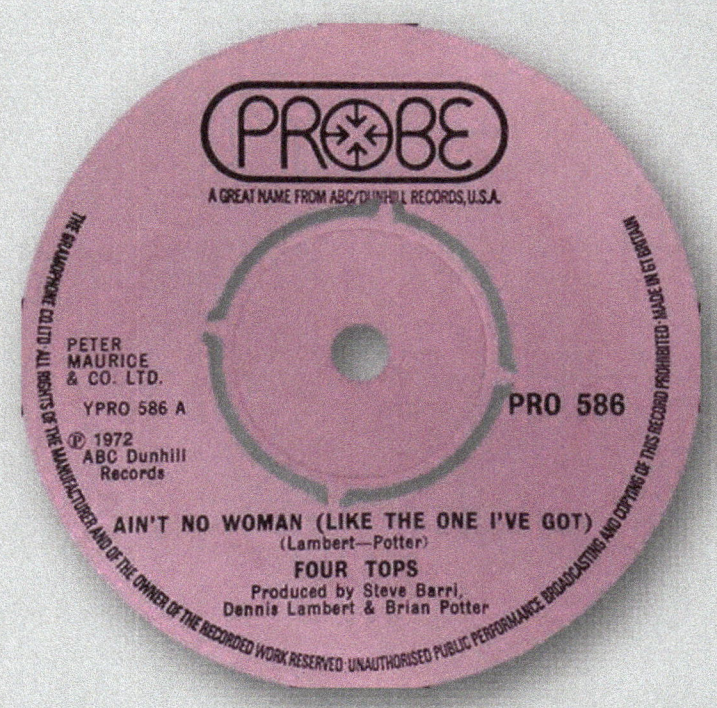

where it secured No.1 in April 1973, earning a gold record.

In Britain, however, it was a slightly different story. 'Keeper' had faired reasonably well, reaching No.18 in the charts, but somewhat surprisingly, this follow-up failed to register despite descent reviews – *"This particularly lovely languid Friends Of Distinction-ish slowie is deservedly a US smash, and deservedly rushed here despite another recent Probe release"* – 'Record Mirror'.

As 1973 progressed, The Four Tops continued to be in the public eye as the switch to Dunhill continued to prove positive, with the Potter/Lambert combination conjuring up a hat-trick of hits, Stateside wise at least, with the Tops third single release on the label '**Are You Man Enough**' b/w '**Piece Of Mind**', released in May.

Once again, the quartet stormed up the American charts, reaching No.2 R&B and No.15 Pop, but again they were seemingly ignored by those one-time fanatic British followers.

Sales of 'Are You Man Enough' were helped by its inclusion in the film 'Shaft In Africa', while it was also to feature in the '**Main Street People**' album, which saw release in September 1973.

"The Tops are hotter than ever and this new collection could not have come about at a better time. The group's recent successes on their new label have been keeping them in the Top Ten and it looks as if there's more of the same coming up in the future based on the high quality of this LP.

"Included, naturally, is their smash, 'Are You Man Enough' from "Shaft In Africa," but that's only the curtain raiser. Other potential singles include 'Am I My Brother's Keeper,' 'Too Little, Too Late' and 'It Won't Be The First Time.' *The harmonies are sweeter than ever as the Tops seem to get even more mellow with age. A great collection destined for the top"* was how the reviewer in 'Cashbox' saw the album.

As a matter of interest, the album included an 'intro' version of 'Main Street People' sung by Lawrence Payton, as well as a different cut, with Levi Stubbs on lead. Payton was also to take the lead on 'Am I My Brothers Keeper'.

In the eyes, or ears of the reviewer in 'Record Mirror', it was that forementioned track and 'Are You Man Enough' that rescued the album, as the remaining tracks were considered "sluggish" and "dire".

Having such a prize asset on their books Dunhill, or perhaps that should read ABC/Dunhill, were determined to get as much mileage out of the guys as they possibly could, without going completely overboard.

There was, however, something of a saturation of the groups material on the record store shelves, especially in the U.K. as Motown, despite having more or less banished the group into their history books released two further singles by them in 1973.

It was obvious that they were simply cashing in on the groups continuing recording career, plus their work on the 'Shaft In Africa' soundtrack, as they released two further recordings – '**So Deep Within You**' b/w '**Happy (Is A Bumpy Road)**' and '**I Can't Quit Your Love**' b/w '**I Am Your Man**'.

The former had been recorded at the same time as 'A Simple Game' back in 1970 and was another Mike Pinder composition and had appeared on the Moody Blues 'Threshold Of A Dream' album. It had also featured on the 'Motown Sound Volume One' album, where it was picked up by DJs on both sides of the Atlantic, hence its release as a single.

The 'B' side had featured in the States on the reverse of 'I Can't Quit Your Love', but the U.K. release of the track from the 'Nature Planned It' album saw 'I Am Your Man', another extracted from that album, on the flip.

As summer 1973 blended into autumn, ABC/Dunhill repeated their previous ideas, taking a similar path to what had proved a thorn in the side of the group at Motown and delved into their current album for their next single, releasing the Obie and Valadia Benson, Ivy Hunter co-penned '**Sweet Understanding Love**' b/w '**Main Street People**'.

Having failed somewhat to capture the imagination of the U.K. record buyers since re-locating to ABC/Dunhill, they finally managed to get back on track with this latest release, which was to reach No.29 in the charts, nine places short of what 'Keeper Of The Castle' had achieved the previous year.

Perhaps the resurgence in interest, over and above their long-standing fan base, was due to a U.K. tour with former Motown stablemates The Detroit Spinners.

Reviews were plentiful and complementary, but to emphasize that the boys had not lost any of their considerable talent or professionalism, it is perhaps best defined by Barrie Williams in the 'Kent Evening Post'. Having extolled the performance of The Spinners, saying that they were "*so polished and enjoyable that they left the Four Tops with a nasty case of "Follow That".*" He continued: "*And they did – with a vengeance,*

- 71 -

proving they are still the undisputed masters of the Detroit sound with which so many people identify.

"The Four Tops put so much effort, obvious enjoyment and vitality into every phrase and every movement that it seems churlish and bad mannered not to join 'the party' – as you're frequently invited to do so.

"Certainly, a night to remember. It seemed pertinent to ponder on just where Messrs. Bowie and Glitter will be in 15 years' time."

Working with Potter and Lambert gave the Tops something of a new lease of life, allowing them to enjoy a freedom that they had not previously experienced at Motown, writing and producing along with creating their own publishing company *"It was, a whole new type of recording venture for us"* exclaimed Duke.

Arguably, the best track on that 'Main Street People' album was the Lambert/Potter penned **'I Just Can't Get You Out Of My Mind'** b/w **'Am I My Brother's Keeper'**, which was released Stateside at the tail end of 1973 – "The Tops are starting '74 with a disk [sic] that none of us will be able to get out of our minds for some time to come. Possessing of that same driving feel as their smash 'Keeper Of The Castle' and 'Are You Man Enough', this power packed track has that same hit potential and should get the year off on the right foot for the Tops, a top group if there ever was one" – 'Cashbox'.

In the U.K., however, its release early in 1974 proved to be a pointless exercise, as once again, it failed to captivate the British record buyers.

1974 had barely got into its stride when the Four Tops devotees were hit with something completely different, and out of the blue, with the Lawrence Payton solo recording '**One Man Woman**' b/w '**Love Makes You Human**'.

Payton was no stranger in regards to being the front man, as all the Tops had taken the lead at some point in their stage act and on record, but this was the first time that one of the quartet had broken away from his life-long companions and recorded solo.

Reviews were favourable – "*a delightfully gentle ballad*" and, "*this debut track is one that people will find impossible to ignore due to his distinctive vocal style and the high quality of the tune. Soul acceptance is a natural, with pop reaction to follow hot and heavily*". but it was not to signify anything remotely like the break-up of the group as some might have thought and suggested, it was simply an opportunity for Lawrence to spread his wings, as had been mentioned upon the groups departure from Motown.

Although Lambert and Potter were by now involved with Haven Records, a subsidiary of Capitol Records, whilst having sold their own Soldier Music publishing company to ABC/Dunhill, their names still appeared alongside that of The Four Tops as the ABC/Dunhill releases continued to appear.

Although it had been Messrs Lambert and Potter, who had done all the spade work for The Four Tops at ABC/Dunhill, along with contributing five songs to the next album release – '**Meeting Of Minds**', recorded in late 1973 and released in April 1974, other names were to appear amongst the credits, in particular the husband and wife duo of Obi and Val Benson. Lawrence Payton's name was also there.

From the above-mentioned album, ABC/Dunhill released '**One Chain Don't Make No Prison**' b/w '**Turn On The Light Of Your Love**' in March 1974, with the reviewer in Cashbox considering it to be one of the groups best releases, "*due to the extra dash of funk missing from many of their previous outings. "Hard driving makes for hard dancing and a playlist incentive that both pop and R&B markets will be immediately attracted to. Should be Top 5 within two months.*"

Those who bought the records proved the reviewer to be only partly correct, as in only squeezed into the top five at No.3 on the R&B charts whilst failing to penetrate the top forty pop. Again, the U.K. voted it a 'miss'.

As for that 'Meeting of The Minds' album, although it did virtually nothing chart wise, it once again proved the versatility of the group. "*A continuation of the perfection that has been the groups trademark*" one review proclaimed, while another echoed much of the same: "*Another outstanding set from this group that appears to reach across all popular musical boundaries. Their greatest strength is still their fine harmony singing, and three of the four members share lead singing through various stages of this set. Excellent production offers large, big band sound that still does not get in the way of the group. Highlights of the LP are still the areas where the three backup voices bounce off the powerful lead voice.*"

Next up was '**Midnight Flower**' b/w '**All My Love**', the 'B' side being another Obie and Val Benson composition, but again the interest just wasn't there when it came to sales.

'Midnight Flower' was also to see release in the U.K., on ABC, but for some unknown reason, it was put out as the 'B' side to 'The Well Is Dry', another track of the 'Meeting Of The Mind' album.

It could be considered that ABC/Dunhill just couldn't get records by The Four Tops out into the marketplace quick enough despite the distinct lack of sales. 'Midnight Flower' made it two singles and an album by the summer of 1974 and before the year was out, another album '**Live & In Concert**' was vying for shelf space in the record stores – a miss-match of titles with a medley that included 'Reach Out', 'Standing In The Shadows Of Love' and 'Baby I Need Your Loving', with the curtain coming down with 'I Can't Help Myself'.

Despite the lack of chart success, theatre and night clubs could still be filled to capacity when 'The Four Tops' was emblazoned across the advertising posters, perhaps in the knowledge that those hits of yesteryear would be heard. But despite the lack of hit records, there was no complaints voiced by the group, at least in public, in regards to this.

"*It was fun working with those guys. They were great writers; great producers and they loved harmony*" commented Duke. "*That made us happy. We could write. We had our own publishing company, the first time we ever had that. That made us extremely happy. That was exciting. It was like a whole new type of recording venture for us.*"

1975 saw things slow down somewhat when it came to record releases, as perhaps ABC/Dunhill began to realise that the marriage between the record company and the group was beginning to reach the end of the road.

June 1975 saw the release of the '**Night Lights Harmony**' album, which featured only one Lambert/Potter track, with the

"As far as records are concerned that happens every day" added Levi. "It's part of the business.

"I don't feel despaired because I know one day we'll sell records... in fact, we do now. We just don't have number one's like we used to have, you know strings of 'ern."

Duke wouldn't accept that the move towards a softer soul sound, like that of The Stylistics and the Chi-Lites had harmed the Tops chances of further chart success, throwing in the hard-hitting owerhouse soul that Harold Melvin and The Bluenotes and The Isley Brothers favoured at present, adding: "I guess it's just a matter of finding the right tune to start a string of things. As Levi says, we're not dying, but being record selling artists we'd certainly like to have some more number ones.

"We sold more records while we were with Motown but we're much better off since we've been by ourselves. It's given us much more scope."

He continued: "For nine years' we were in a place where we couldn't develop in that category because we had producers and writers who were doing so well.

"They were some of the most beautiful days I've ever had in my life, but no, I wouldn't go back."

Levi, however, interrupted to add: "Under different circumstances we might,"

"Why?" echoed Duke. "We did pretty well there and we're still getting paid for services rendered. in fact, we're getting more now than we did when we were there."

majority of the others seeing Lawrence Payton being co-credited, as well as assistant producer alongside Steve Barri.

Single wise, there would be only two, with all four sides gleaned from the album – '**Seven Lonely Nights**' b/w '**I Can't Hold On Much Longer**' and '**We All Gotta Stick Together**' b/w '**Drive Me Out Of My Mind**'. Both appearing on ABC, not ABC/Dunhill.

Despite the lack of chart success in the U.K., The Four Tops never forgot, nor neglected their fan base across the Atlantic and whilst on British soil in Late 1975, they opened their soul in a 'Record Mirror & Disc" interview.

"Of course It bothers us that recently our hits have died off," said Duke. "Not that we're egotistical, but we know that we do have a record market and we should be selling much more records than we are.

"I don't know quite where to lay the blame right now but I'm sure we'll work it out by the middle of 1976. "Fortunately, we do have an immediate public we can work to and we do work to - like, 90 per cent houses."

1976 saw Payton again behind the controls and the microphone, working on the '**Catfish**' album, with the title track being described as "a whimsical disco-boogie fish-fry tune", while Payton himself was to add that the opportunity to work on the production side of things was "*the chance of a lifetime*", adding: "*We needed to do something that black people could hook up with, we had always sung pop music before.*"

And so, 1976 finally saw The Four Tops embrace 'disco'. Some felt that it was only a matter of time, as their past sojourns into the recording studio had seen them cover everything else, from Broadway standards, R&B, pop and the dance floor fillers of the pre-glitter-ball era, but whether their, let's say, rejection of the 'Saturday Night Fever' scene was deliberate or otherwise, they finally enticed the disco generation with '**Catfish**', penned by Bridges, Payton and Farrow – "*A disco single with a very suggestive story line about a dancer whose talents make a man's nature rise!!*"

The single, with '**Drive Me Out Of My Mind**' on the 'B' side, only made No.7 in the R&B chart and a disappointing No.71 pop.

Why it failed to go higher remains something of a mystery. Were they considered 'dated' by the current teenage market?

It certainly wasn't due to the reviews, or indeed the musicians who backed the quartet in the studio, with the sleeve notes revealing the likes of Earl Van Dyke, Dennis Coffey, Eddie 'Bongo' Brown and Gil Askey were all on board, due to it being partly recorded at the United Sound Systems studios in Detroit.

"*The Tops wrote most of the material and where it lacks the urgency of some of their earlier work, the harmonies are smooth. The melodies are good, but not brilliant.*" Coupled with "*The Four Tops are noted for putting out solid, satisfying R&B records, and this is no exception.*

"*From the first cut "Catfish" exudes an air of excitement that will be hard to beat on radio and in the stores. ABC has a big fall sales programme underway, so retailers can be assured of constant support on this one. 'Strung Out For Your Love' and 'Feel Free' are two cuts that will appeal immediately to R&B programmers. A catalogue push of the Four Tops past work, in conjunction with this fine new album, would not be a bad idea*", could be found amongst the reviews.

When asked about 'Catfish' Duke replied: "*We thought it was a great song*", going on to explain the story behind it: "*We were down in New Orleans around Mardi Gras time. Lawrence ran into this girl and was sitting around the bar with her all day. At night they went out dancing. He came back about four in the morning and said to me, "Duke, I just had the baddest woman in the world". I said "Great man. Good for you. I'm going back to sleep. Next day he was writing this song about "Catfish makes my nature rise". It was clever.*"

Clever perhaps it was, but some radio stations didn't rise to the bait and kept it off their play-lists, which perhaps severely diluted the chance of it becoming a major hit, while some of the fanbase were to consider it to be beneath the group.

Another disco loaded track on the album 'Disco Daddy' was poor by comparison and one of those immediately forgettable cuts.

Despite the decade still having four years to run, 'Catfish' would be the last 'hit' of the seventies a peculiar period in the history of the

group and one that would never have been envisaged back in those rose-tinted days in Detroit.

As one of the numerous reviewers had suggested, '**Feel Free**' b/w '**You Know You Like It**' and '**Strung Out For Your Love**' b/w '**You Can't Hold Back On Love**' were the strongest tracks other than the title one, but it was still something of a surprise that ABC decided to release them as singles, with the album being regarded as a failure.

The former of the pair was the last release of 1976, the latter, the first of 1977, one of only two releases that year, as the ABC period began to stagger to is finale.

Confusion, however would reign for those who picked up their copy of 'Record Mirror' for December 3rd 1977, as reviewer John Shearlow committed a cardinal sin, by not doing his homework. His musical interests were obviously far removed from that of The Four Tops, as he penned the following as his opening lines in his review of the album: "*An apt enough title for the venerable Tops, already incorporating a second-generation Levi Stubbs (as in Jnr) into their line-up.*

"*Yessir, after something like 20 years in the soul - vending business Three Tops just wouldn't have sounded right*."

Had the British public/fan base missed something? Had events Stateside not crossed the Atlantic as yet? No. Shearlow had seen Levi named as 'Levi Stubbs jnr' as he often was in articles and such like and simply presumed that Levi's son had stepped in behind the microphone!

His review continued: "*And really (plainly and honestly now) neither does this album. There's still polished shoes and dinner jacket class oozing out of the grooves - there certainly isn't a track that could be accused of arid indulgence.*

"*But instead of hitting where it hurts with dynamic harmony, 'The Show Must Go On' holds together with the faded elegance of the immortal line Itself.*

"*When they reach out and actually do get there, as with a nostalgically controlled and powerful version of Stephen Bishop's near classic 'Save It For A Rainy Day', It looks salt the light Is still flickering.*

"*Yet for the most part the liaison with producer Lawrence Payton (plus a frightening bevy of distinguished sessioneers) results in a routinised weld of tired but clever vocals onto studio thump 'n' funk.*

"*Eight songs and eight different approaches maybe; but from the lengthy 'Love Is A Joy' to the snappy 'Runnin' From Love' It's music from the shadows And that ain't right.*"

At least his review was correct!

1977 was to see the release of the aptly entitled album '**The Show Must Go On**', the title track also appearing as a single, which was once again recorded at Detroit's United Sound, Pro Studio and produced by Lawrence Payton, who also co-penned three of the tracks, taking lead on 'Love Is A Joy'. Gil Askey and Earl Van Dyke were again involved, while another name of interest creeps into the credits, Ronnie McNeir, which appears alongside that of Obi Benson on the tracks 'I Can't live Without You' and 'You'll Never Find A Better Man'. But more about Mr McNeir later.

January 1978 was to create some excitement in regards to the groups recording career, something that had arguably been missing in recent times, when an article in 'Billboard' revealed that the group were re-uniting with Messrs Holland-Dozier-Holland, "*At least for one LP*" announced Duke Fakir, who was also to admit that the group had lost some of its popularity.

"We got Holland-Dozier-Holland back together to do one LP for us. "We're going back to our old type of recording. This LP will be a totally contemporary effort with the producers that we worked best with in all our recording years."

Mentioning that there had been litigation going on among the trio, Duke added: "We have worked out a way for this merger to be done and we're starting the LP immediately.

"We're planning to create a Four Tops 'now' sound that we have been missing for some time. And we feel Holland-Dozier-Holland can do it.

"We sat down and tried to determine in what direction we would take our music – if we should go toward the Commodores sound, the Earth, Wind and Fire sound or back to the old Tops sound. We decided to go with a mixture of what we sounded like ten years ago and put new feelings and some extra touches to it."

In the article, Duke was also to reveal that the group had taken to managing themselves. "We know just about all the promoters and club owners and we have made some good friends. So, we go directly to them. We don't even have a booking agent.

"We just let them know that we're available and we co-ordinate the dates.

"Because we haven't been in demand for concert tours in the U.S. the offers we are getting in the U.S. we are not taking now because we know we're not hot and it wouldn't be a successful venture. We only want to go where we know we are going to draw as opposed to just being out there."

Re-uniting with the Holland – Dozier - Holland team would not be immediate, far from it, but the show did go on, although it was to be twelve months down the line, the

curtain finally came down on the Four Tops ABC career with the release of the album '**The Four Tops At The Top**', recorded in Philadelphia's Sigma Sound Studios.

In the opinion of many, time was catching up with The Four Tops, if indeed it had already not done so. Music, as it always had done was evolving more and more, new acts were appearing on the scene with mind numbing regularity, and in all honesty, mere amateurs when comparison was made to the likes of Detroit's finest.

In regards to this latest album, the quartet were considered "*as vocally powerful as ever*" according to the reviewer in 'Billboard', but, in recent times, there was always a "but" and they went on to write: "*However, it appears that the Tops have gotten stale. While material is good, the group often sounds dated.*
"*On the other hand, it takes on a number of U.K. hit records for the likes of The Yardbirds, The Hollies and Herman's Hermits. None of that magic, however, was to rub off on The Four Tops with the 1977 recording 'For Your Love' b/w ''You'll Never Find A Better Man'*

fresh sound when different members are placed in lead roles.

"*Instrumentation is both small band and large orchestral. Best cuts: 'H.E.L.P.', 'Bits And Pieces', Seclusion' and 'Just In Time'.*"

The reviewer did get his assumptions correct in picking out '**H.E.L.P.**' as being one of the best cuts, as ABC released it as a single b/w '**Inside A Broken Man**'. The Four Tops final release on the label in November 1978.

On the parting of the ways, Levi Stubbs was to comment: "*They never took the time and effort for us. They wanted something for nothing, but even a group as successful as we were, has to be continually marketed. We lost a lot of records like that at ABC. We also felt that maybe the company was more geared to breaking white acts like Steely Dan at that time.*"

Before moving on, it is worth mentioning one or two other releases on ABC that did not see any action in the States.

Firstly, from the pen of Graham Gouldman, bass player and co-lead singer with 10cc, who had previously penned a considerable number of U.K. hit records for the likes of The Yardbirds, The Hollies and Herman's Hermits. None of that magic, however, was to rub off on The Four Tops with the 1977 recording '**For Your Love**' b/w ''**You'll Never Find A Better Man**' and released as both a 7" and 12" single.

1977 also produced '**Put It In The News**' b/w '**When Your Dreams Take Wings And Fly**', which was also released as a 7" and a 12" single, with a special double 'A' side DJ edited version also available.

A year earlier there was '**Let Me Know The Truth**' b/w '**Seven Lonely Nights**', released in Spain.

As mentioned at the start, this is no definitive story, not every recording or release is mentioned, far from it, but before bringing the curtain down on the ABC/Dunhill years, let's mention two other releases from 1976, double 'A' sides, which were also released back-to-back in 1975 – '**I'm Glad You Walked Into My Life' (Dedicated To Stevie)**' and '**Mama You're All Right With Me**'. The 'A' sides being in mono, the 'B' side in stereo.

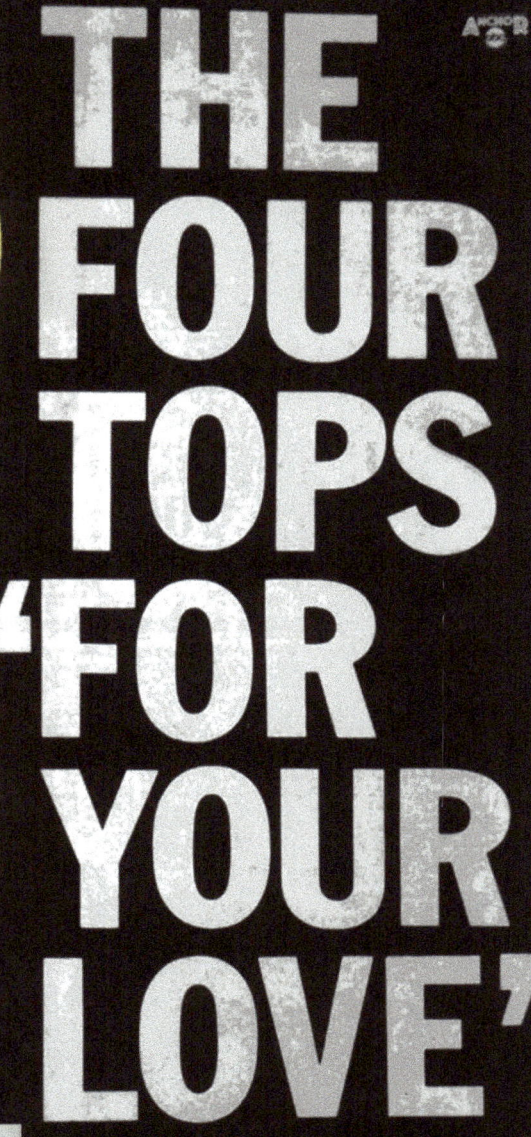

ONLY THE STRONG SURVIVE

'Only The Strong Survive' was recorded by Jerry Butler in 1968 and taken from his 'The Ice Man' album and released as a single the following year. Then, 1977 saw Billy Paul attack the charts with his version, which was ever so slightly modified and saw the lyric line change to – "*Only the strong survive, only the strong survive, weak fall by the wayside.*
"*You gotta be strong, you gotta hold on, you gotta keep goin' on...*"

It was a song that the Four Tops should have featured in their vast repertoire, or at least in their theatre shows, as those words from the Billy Paul version emphasised the group perfectly.

1978 had seen the foursome cut their ties with ABC/Dunhill, but that parting of the ways could well have come seven months earlier, in late April of that year. It could also have signified the end of the Four Tops full stop.

On the wet and windy Tuesday night of April 25th, the group were around fifteen miles out of Athens, Georgia, heading for South Carolina, having fulfilled their booking at the B&L Warehouse, thrilling yet another packed house.

Suddenly, a truck swerves across the lanes and collides with a Trailway bus, nudging it down and embankment, where it came to rest amongst some bushes. Fourteen of those on board were injured, including Levi, who required six stitches in a leg wound and Obie, who suffered a fractured jaw. Duke and Lawrence were more fortunate, sustaining relatively minor cuts and bruises.

"*We thank god that we're still alive*" commented Levi.

Levi and Obie were left in peace to recuperate from their injuries, while Duke and Lawrence enjoyed an unscheduled break from their often-tiring commitments. But, in true troubadour fashion, it was not long before they were back on the road performing,

Fully recovered, both physically and mentally, they were soon back to what many would have considered a gruelling schedule, performing both at home and abroad. Had that accident brought fatalities, then their immortality was assured, as they were one of the stand-out acts within the world of not just Soul/R&B music, but pop music as a whole.

Although lauded in America, it was in Britain that they maintained a vast fan-base, with the music correspondents in local and national newspapers regularly singing their praises when a tour schedule brought them to town.

Ray King of the 'Manchester Evening News' was to write in the

Crumpled Bus That 'The Four Tops' Singing Group Was Riding In

Friday October 24th 1980 edition: "Of *all the American soul groups that dominated the dance music of the Sixties, Detroit's Four Tops are the most unashamedly nostalgic; 90 percent of their Golden Garter set last night was drawn from their repertoire of classic Motown hits. Indeed, they have done little noteworthy on disc since.*

"*Lead singer Levi Stubbs proved last night that every Motown group had within its rank a true and talented stylist. Alone among his contemporaries he stayed in the ranks while Diana Ross, Eddie Kendricks, Smokey Robinson and Ben E King carved out considerable solo careers.*

"*Constant repetition over the years has knocked some of the finer points off the songs, but the quartet still generate considerable excitement with a non-stop show.*

"*Those who were mods the first time around loved every minute.*"

A couple of years down the line and it was much of the same. Katy Carpenter told the readers of 'The Stage' what they had missed at the Hammersmith Odeon.

"*After performing together for a staggering twenty-seven years, the Four Tops have not surprisingly come up with an entertainment package guaranteed to please.*

"*It is as slick and well-groomed as the band themselves in their dazzling white suits, pressed to perfection, and it is exactly what their fans want and expect. If you like your pop squeaky clean, the Four Tops will send you home humming.*

"*They bounced on stage at Hammersmith Odeon with the enthusiastic energy of newcomers. Before the eager audience had time to blink, they were hurtling through that early Motown hit, "Baby, I Need Your Loving".*

"*Backed by an impressive orchestra, they kept the hits flowing at an alarming rate delivering their golden oldies in a frenzied burst of nostalgia: "Ain't No Woman Like The One I've Got", "Reach Out, I'll Be There", "Same Old Song" and "Standing In The Shadow of Love".*

"*By now the audience were out of their seats and dancing in the aisles as Levi Stubbs delivered the songs in his powerful style and the remaining Tops demonstrated their ability to sing in harmony while going through a complicated, if highly rehearsed, dance routine.*

"*Then it was time to promote their newer material, no less appreciated by the fans who were ready to clap along to anything. They gave "When She Was My Girl" twice, judging their audience with uncanny precision.*

"*The label of MOR is as firmly attached to The Four Tops as Motown once was, and there is nothing unexpected in their performance. But their fans will go on buying their hits as long as they keep churning out that well-established, instantly recognisable formula, which has deservedly kept them at the top for so long.*"

Getting back on the road was never going to be a problem, as they were now capably managed by Ron Strasner, who had been associated with Rare Earth, Funkadelic and Martha Reeves in the 1970's, but returning to the recording studio was far from straight forward, as they were now without a recording contract and continued to be without one when the new decade arrived.

There was no need to hawk a CV around the record companies, as their reputation went before them and several companies showed an interest in signing them up.

In early 1982, it looked as though they would be teaming up with the Jerry Love/Michael Zager duo, but the negotiations stumbled to a close with an agreement failing to be reached. "It's their loss" countered Love.

But as one door closed, another opened and a chance meeting between Strasner and the wife of producer David Wolfest was to see a meeting arranged between the two men.

Wolfest, like Strasner had been very much involved in the music of the 1970's as a writer, guitarist and producer for a host of names, ranging from General Johnson to Don Covay to Melissa Manchester and at the time of the meeting was a staff producer with Casablanca Records via The Entertainment Company.

Having got together, a further meeting was arranged, this time along with composers Marc Blatte and Larry Gottljeb, which in turn lead to '**When She Was My Girl**' b/w '**Something To Remember**', which was released in the autumn of 1981.

Speaking in regards to the deal with Casablanca, Levi was to say: "*We were offered good deals by a number of labels, but we were particularly interested in getting guarantees that we would receive a real promotion and marketing effort. That was just as important to us as the money part.*" He was also quick to praise Dave Wolfert for his integral part in settling quickly at Casablanca and hitting the ground running with what was instant success.

"*He's intelligent, knows what he's doing, knows what he's looking for and listens to us.* "*It turned out good for us because the group had a lot of say, but not contrary to what Dave Wolfert ultimately thought. He was the producer and we let him produce.*"

Having been around for so long, he was also more than aware of things change and had changed over the years.

Levi continued: "*We're not kids. We realise that the record market is geared to younger people in a lot of record company minds, so for us it's definitely a challenge.*"

If you had never set eyes on the actual record and were hearing the song '**When She Was My Girl**' for the first time, only being told that it was The Four Tops, then you would have been more than justified in saying that this was a Motown recording.

It didn't have the pulsating beat of the Holland-Dozier-Holland era, but it had everything else and it was of little surprise that it hit No.1 in the Stateside R&B charts, while No.11 on the pop chart listing, plus hitting the No.3 spot in the U.K., earning a silver disc, certainly did not signify failure.

With Obie's bass-line of "boom-dee-boom-boom" of 'When She Was My Girl'

still being sung and heard, the group saw the release of their first album on the Casablanca label – '**Tonight**'.

Despite the 'Cashbox' review reading: "*Still intact after a prestigious 28-year career, The Four Tops add to their legend with "Tonight." The album still has some of the touches of Motown days gone by and songs like "Baby I Need Your Loving," "Reach Out, I'll Be There" and "Standing In The Shadows Of Love;" and producer David Wolfert has given these Detroit - born soul stirrers a new contemporary edge that should put them back on top of the charts. Levi Stubbs proves he still has some of the grittiest and most emotional vocal chops around*", the rest of the album except for one track, the infectious drag you out of your seat and onto the dancefloor sound of 'Don't Walk Away' unfortunately did not live up to the to the expectations create by that initial release, but Casablanca followed 'When She Was My Girl' with two further tracks gleaned from it, with '**Let Me Set You Free**' in November 1981 and '**Tonight I'm Gonna Love You All Over**' in January

1982. That latter track reaching No.43 in the U.K.

Somewhat strangely, they did not consider it worthwhile in releasing '**Don't Walk Away**' b/w '**I'll Never Leave Again**' in the States, but did give it a release in Europe, Australia and South Africa, being justified with a No.16 placing in Britain, although it could be argued that it deserved much higher. Then again, perhaps not if you went by the review in 'Record Mirror' by a female who looked more at home with bands the likes of Altered Images and The Waitresses – to whom she gave 'record of the week', as she penned: "*Rather mundane follow-up to 'When She Was My Girl'. Mind you, that was hardly the most memorable thing. I've ever heard.*"

Casablanca were to release a second album '**One More Mountain**' and once again, pulling a track from it for a single release – '**I Believe In You And Me**' b/w '**Sad Hearts**', a minor hit. 'I Believe In You And Me' was scheduled for release as a 'B' side for '**Givin' It Up**', which was never to see the light of day. Another track – '**Nobody's Gonna Love You Like I Do**' b/w '**Sad Hearts**' saw release in Holland.

Of the single 'I Believe In You And Me', Marc Taylor, in his excellent publication 'A Touch Of Classic Soul' was to write that this was "*considered by many to be Levi's best vocal performance on vinyl, as his voice glides from baritone to tenor, and it remains a wedding day staple and the groups finest ballad.*"

Tucked away in amongst those Casablanca releases was one on the RSO label '**Back To School Again**', from the soundtrack of 'Grease 2', which failed to hit the top fifty, either in the U.S. or U.K.

Life at Casablanca came to an end in the spring of 1982, following the death of the labels founder and its current chairman Neil Bogart.

BACK WHERE THEY BELONG

Although The Four Tops had vowed never to split up, we have already seen Lawrence Payton branch out on his own and in 1982, now it was the turn of Levi Stubbs to step forward, not to record a solo single, but to record a duet – 'I Wanna Make It Up To You' with long-time friend Aretha Franklin for her 'Jump To It' album. Needless to say, his three friends were not far away, as they could be found on backing vocals.

1983 saw Motown celebrate its 25th anniversary, with Suzanne de Passe producing a two-hour television special under the title - 'Yesterday, Today, Forever', which brought together the majority of artists who had helped give the label its global appeal, to perform at the Pasadena Civic Auditorium in California.

In typical, modern-day fashion, there were many omissions from the list of performers, or indeed from the invited guests. There was no Kim Weston or Marvelettes. No Edwin Starr or Velvelettes. No Brenda Holloway or Jimmy Ruffin. No Marv Johnson or Gladys Knight. Their omissions were even more disappointing and hurtful when you consider that the likes of Adam Ant and Linda Ronstadt, neither of whom had any Motown connection whatsoever featured.

It was later revealed that James Jamerson, a key member of the Funk Brothers and whose guitar licks are so audible on numerous Motown recordings, had to pay for a ticket!

The celebration, which could have been billed as a wake, remembering those missing performers, was completely dominated by Michael Jackson's 'moonwalk', which was to attract just about as much attention as the definitive moonwalk itself.

But despite all the omissions, The Four Tops were there, had they not been, serious questions would have been asked, appearing on-stage with The Temptations, in what was billed as "a duel". From 'Reach Out I'll Be There', 'Baby I Need Your Loving', 'I Can't Help Myself', into 'Ain't Too Proud To Beg', 'Get Ready' and 'My Girl'.

The only winner on the night was the audience, but it ignited a flame that was to see the two groups take a similar show on the road, touring across America and Europe on a regular basis, with featured guest acts. One night the Tops would headline, the next it would be the turn of the Temptations and on it went.

Uniting with The Temptations was not simply confined to theatres and the like, as it also took the two groups into the studio, with The Temptations doing backing on another McLeod/Bolton production 'Hang', then amid rumours that they were about to become part of

the Motown organisation, came news of a promo LP **'The Battle Of The Champions'**, with the two groups combining on the track 'The Battle Song (I'm The One)', with each group then contributing a further four tracks each.

The early eighties would also see a couple of releases that were recorded when the group were between labels, prior to re-signing for Motown, recordings that might well have slipped below the radar. **'I'm Here Again'** b/w **'I'm Here Again (Instrumental)'** on the Detroit based 'Reliant Entertainment Group' label, the first release from this company and was described as "*a 12" dance single*" and "*a heavy, funky record with a strong beat, heavy electronics, coupled with a grunting chorus and raw vocals from Stubbs.*"

There was also talk of an album, and a further five songs are known about, but.....

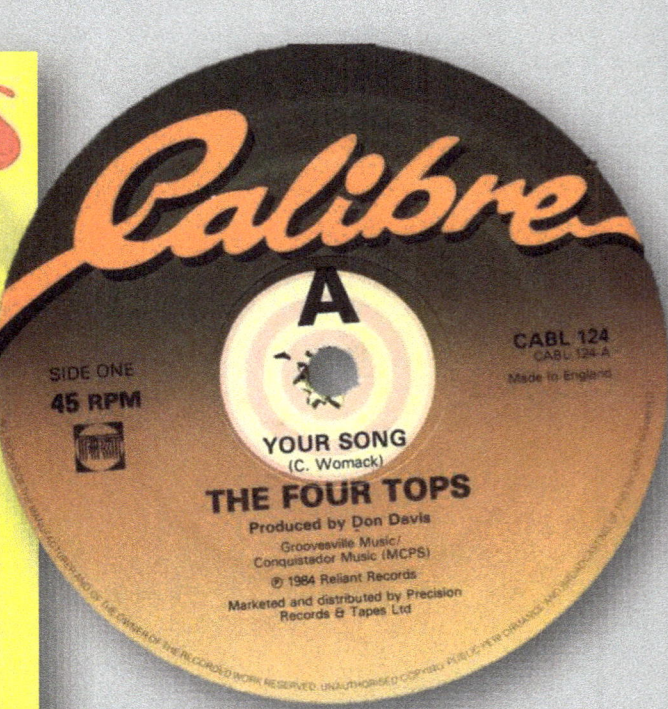

The second recording appeared on the Calibre label, the disco/electro sub-label of Pye Records, who had also released recordings by The Real Thing, Young & Company and Kelly Marie.

Released in 1984, this was the Cecil Womack composed, Don Davis produced '**Your Song**' b/w the afore mentioned '**I'm Here Again**'.

Saying that there were two recordings from the early eighties is perhaps not entirely correct, as there was a third, again from the spring of 1984 which can be found on a 'YouTube' video clip.

"Artists Help "Do It In Detroit"" was the headline of a 'Billboard' article which went on to read: -"Do It In Detroit," an image-building campaign for the Motor City recently instituted by Mayor Coleman Young, has made music a significant part of its promotional effort. The Four Tops and Sammy Davis Jr. have both recorded songs in honor of this city.

"The Four Tops, all of whom still reside in Detroit, recorded "Be A Part Of The Heart Of Detroit," which was used to kick off the "Do It In Detroit" campaign. The song was written by Paul Hoffman, Frank Floyd and Bill Lane, and arranged by the Entertainment Co.'s David Wolfert (who produced the Four Tops hit When She Was My Girl'), all of whom donated their services. It has a sound reminiscent of the classic line as that on the Supremes' "Can't Hurry Love."

"The Four Tops recorded the song in two takes the night prior to the Major's formal announcement of the campaign. "When you believe in something, it just sort of comes naturally," says lead singer Levi Stubbs.

"We were very pleased to record a song about our city."

"Be A Part Of The Heart Of Detroit" is heard in the city's discos, bars, and at intermission at sporting and cultural events. Local stations are playing the song as part of their public service broadcasting time. Detroit's top black/urban station, WJLB, is now promoting itself with the ad line - "Do It In Detroit With WJLB." The city's newspapers and television stations are donating space and airtime to publicizing the campaign. A video version of "Heart Of Detroit," highlighting city scenery, is being played on local television and the Four Tops have talked of shooting a video version of their own.

"The popularity of "Heart Of Detroit" has generated interest among other Detroit entertainers in the campaign. Aretha Franklin, a full-time resident of the Motor City for several years, is said to be interested in cutting a version of the tune, perhaps with the Tops' Stubbs.

"Cassette copies of the song are being given away for a limited time. City officials and Motown are discussing whether the song will appear on the Tops' next album or as a locally distributed single."

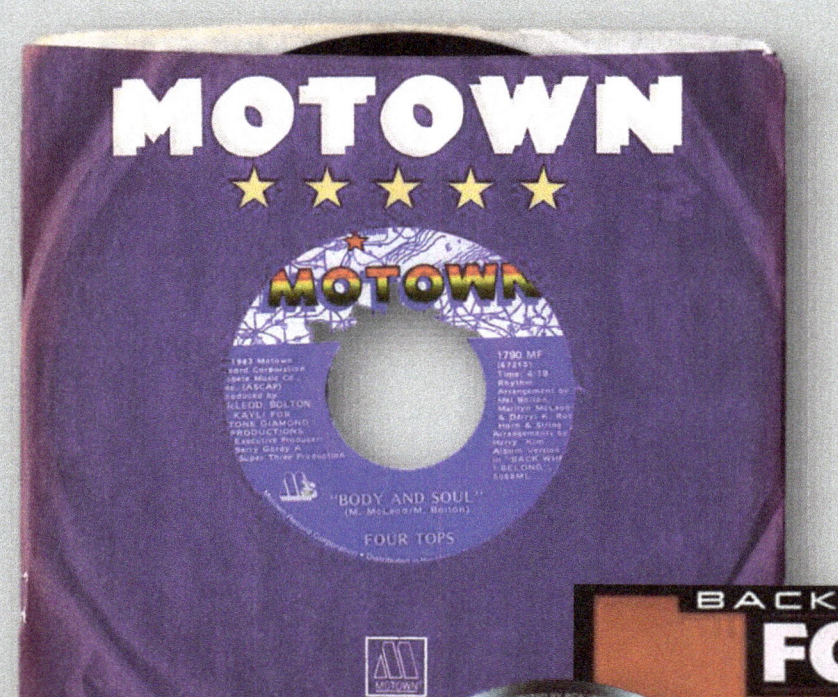

Just Can't Walk Away' b/w 'Hang', which was to bring smiles all round as it headed straight for the chart, although it was only to peak at No.36 R&B and No. 71 pop, while just managing to break into the U.K. top 100 at No.95.

In regards to the album, the 'Cashbox' review read: "*With its latest single, "I Just Can't Walk Away," entering the Cash Box Black Contemporary Charts in its first week of release, the Four Tops latest LP could bring the rejuvenated line-up some of the glory of old.*"

While that Motown 25th anniversary show had its negatives, there was also positives, with the latter being in The Four Tops return to the Motown stable. Whether they were snared by the bright lights, meeting up with old friends again, or whatever, they signed a contract and walked back through the door that Berry Gordy had said was always open for them.

Following in their footsteps came Brian and Eddie Holland and Lamont Dozier, which was to result in the album '**Back Where I Belong**', or at least one side of it, while Gordy himself, Willie Hutch, Marilyn McLeod, Gil Askey and Mel Bolton took the production credits on the other. Also, back into the studio came James Jamerson alongside a huge rhythm section.

A month prior to the release of that album in October 1983, Motown released something of a 'taster' in '**I**

"All the essential ingredients are there: the strong material, the involvement of Motown hit makers, Edward Holland, Jr., Lamont Dozier and Brian Holland, who write and produce the songs on the first side, and most importantly, the group's powerful singing,

"The album has more upbeat funk songs like 'What Have We Got To Lose', featuring the singing of Aretha Franklin, 'Sail On' and 'Body And Soul' while it still spotlights the groups evocative harmonies on such ballads as the previously mentioned single and the title track, 'Back Where 1 Belong' puts the group back in the spotlight, where it belongs, as well as with its old label where it all began."

Also, from the album came the Holland-Dozier-Holland written and produced 'Make Yourself Right At Home' b/w 'Sing A Song Of Yesterday'.

"The vocal band has again adapted to the times with a driving techno-funk single that fits 1984 perfectly" penned the reviewer in 'Cashbox', adding: "Lead vocalist Levi Stubbs turns in his usual authoritative performance, and the other Tops spin a smooth and seamless backdrop for their leader. Highlighted by some inspired synthesizer work, "Make Yourself Right At Home" articulates what the Four Tops have always done in the music business, and here they do it with typical verve and energy."

Strangely, the 'B' side was a track from the 1970 album 'Changing Times' I suppose they were!

'Body and Soul' [b/w 'Sexy Ways'], a McLeod and Bolton composition, who had also arranged the rhythm section on 'I Just Can't Walk Away', was another track to be sifted off that 'Back Where I Belong' album and released in the spring of 1985, or the following year depending on what country you lived in.

That 'Sexy Ways' track was also to appear on the May 1985 'Magic' album, a mixture of songs from a mixture of writers and produced by Willie Hutch, Johnny Bristol and Hal Davis.

As could be expected, Motown simply couldn't resist the temptation to pull another couple of tracks from the album, releasing 'Don't Tell Me That It's Over' b/w 'I'm Ready For Love', yes, the old Martha and the Vandellas hit. Unfortunately, the Tops couldn't emulate Ms Reeves!

The album also included a cover of the Diana Ross track 'Remember Me'.

It was to be a case of remember me, or remember us, as the second parting of the ways was drawing closer and closer.

Returning to the Motown fold was perhaps not the best decision the group had made and behind closed doors could have voiced their regrets in doing so.

They knew when they left the first

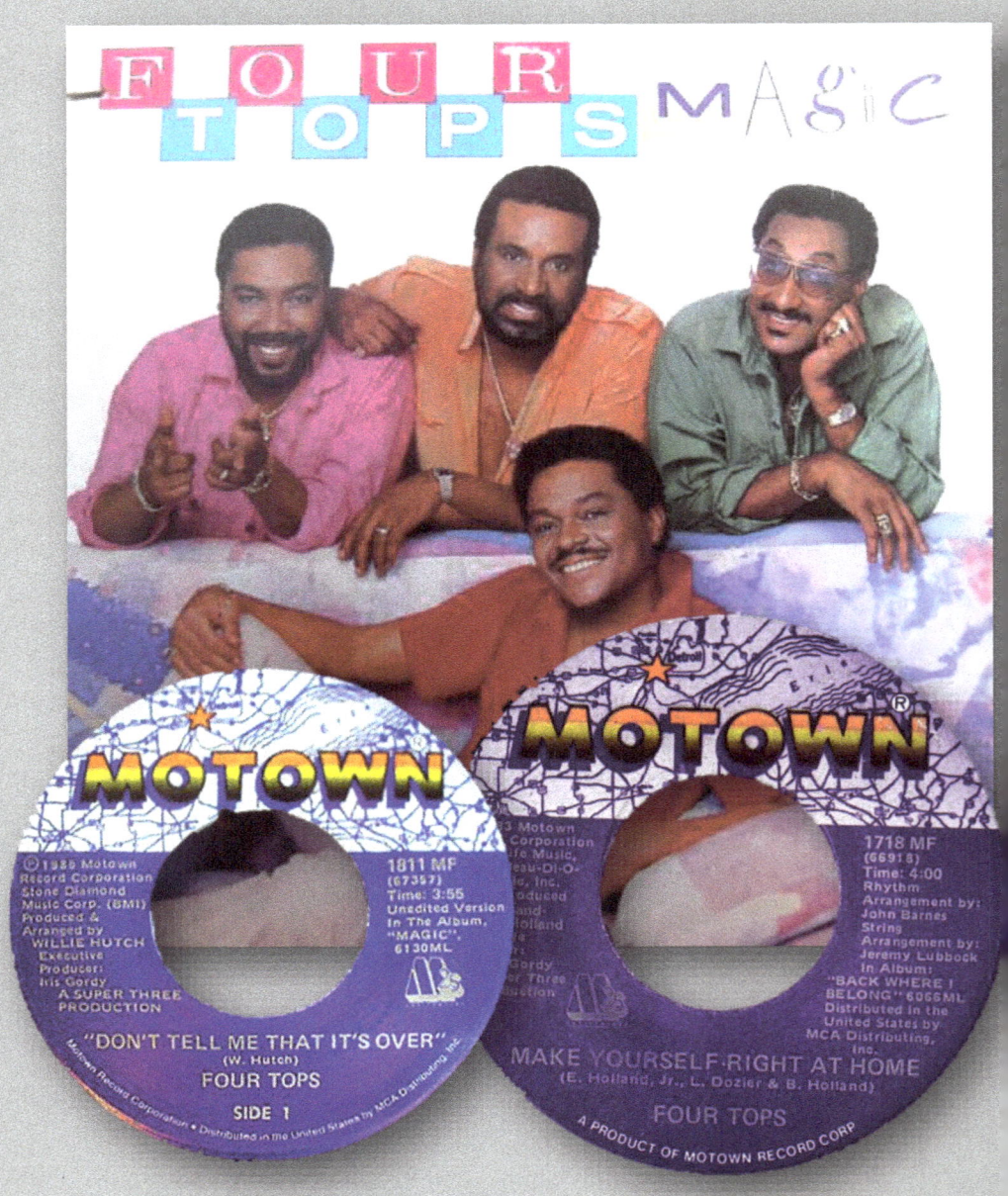

time that the company was changing, evolving into something completely different from those halcyon days of the sixties. The music world itself had changed dramatically and was perhaps not willing to accommodate those elder statesmen, whose fanbase had also aged concurrently. Yes, there was still that strong following, both at home and abroad, but it was not enough to push those singles and albums up the charts like before.

'Don't Tell Me That It's Over' would have been an apt track to bring down the curtain on that second spell at Motown, but there was to be one further release in the summer of 1986 – '**Hot Nights**' b/w '**Again**' or that same 'A' side coupled with '**A Medley Of Hits**'. America seeing the former, while the U.K. was to be blessed with both releases. That eight minute-three seconds of a 'B' side consisting of 'I Can't Help' Myself', 'Shake Me, Wake Me', 'Standing in The Shadows Of Love', 'Reach Out I'll Be There' and 'Bernadette'.

The 'Cashbox' issue of March 8th 1986 reported: "*The Four Tops are set to release a new album tentatively titled 'Indestructible' (Motown)*", with that music papers rival 'Billboard' going one step further the following month, with a more in-depth article accompanied by quotes from Duke Fakir.

It began: "*With Motown preparing to release the group's third album since its return to the label, the Four Tops are not at all content to rest on old laurels. Rather, the durable quartet seeks to re-establish itself as a viable chart act for professionalism if no other reason.* "*For a while it didn't matter that much*," acknowledges lead tenor Duke Fakir. "*But our voices are still there, the motivation is still there, and we feel we're capable of selling records. We just have to find an '80s formula.*

"*Then there are various career benchmarks which have eluded the group. We've never sold a platinum album or won a Grammy, which people take for granted that we've done.*

"*Those are the big motivational factors that we can still attain, because now everyone from 18 to 45 is selling big records. The music is diversified, which means the door is wide open for anything that's good.*"

Now, before going any further into the article/interview, we have to fast forward to July 1986 and 'Billboard's' look at the forthcoming releases – "*Top black releases include Melba Moore's "A Lot Of Love" on Capitol, the Four Tops' "Hot Nights" on Motown; …*"

So, what is it to be, 'Hot Nights' or 'Indestructible'?

As it turned out, it was to be neither, for the time being at least.

So, reversing back to that article/interview, Duke was to freely admit that the right material and production had been lacking since the 1981 release of 'When She Was My Girl' and that the Motown albums that followed "*reverted to the same Motown formula* [of] *going with what the company says, but it didn't work.*" This time, he continues, "*We went back to them and said, 'This is the '80s. The artists with the hit albums - like Stevie Wonder, Lionel Richie, and Rick James - bring in what they have and get the budget that they need. The artist is in control. Berry Gordy said, 'Hey! You're probably right. Let's see what happens.' And we put together a production that we're comfortable with and confident in.*"

"*We returned to what works,*" Duke continued, mentioning the fact that they were now re-united with Dave Wolfert and Steve Barri, who had been

behind the Dunhill 'Keeper Of The Castle' album. "*They knew what we needed, and we knew what we could do. It goes back to the Four Tops' total sound now, not trying to recapture it, but update it, concentrate on one single with a great video to put us in the record market again.*"

The article went on to say that the group hoped to have the single "Indestructive,"[sic] featuring guest vocalist Smokey Robinson, out in advance of the completed but untitled album. If a video is produced on "Indestructible," it will be the Four Tops' first clip not counting their little - remembered "Grease 2" soundtrack effort, "Back To School Again.".

There have been countless references to singers within the lyrics of songs, Dexy's Midnight Runners celebrating both Jackie Wilson, in 1982 and Geno Washington the following year, while Arthur Conley went somewhat overboard on 'Sweet Soul Music'. But if ever a singer deserved to be immortalised in verse, then it was Levi Stubbs and 1986 was to witness that happening when Billy Bragg recorded 'Levi Stubbs' Tears' - "*She takes off the Four Tops tape and puts it back in its case/When the world falls apart some things stay in place/Levi Stubbs' tears run down his face.*"

It's Wikipedia entry saying "*The song's title refers to The Four Tops lead singer Levi Stubbs, whose music remains a source of comfort to the protagonist through years of abandonment, injury, and domestic violence.*"

In regards to Levi, he was to become a film star, of sorts, in 1987,

"A Voice In Hollywood" announced 'Billboard', when he took on the part of Audrey II, a people-eating plant in the film 'Little Shop Of Horrors'.

"*There's talk about the possibility of a sequel, but I'm not taking it seriously,*" Levi was quoted as saying following his screen debut. "*First and foremost, I'm one of the Four Tops, and they were nice enough to let me take time off to do it.*"

Speaking in regards to the project, he initially doubted that he was capable of producing what was required of the role he was asked to fill, in what was often a gruelling period, involving six-day sessions between July and October at Pine Crest Studios in London. It was far removed from the studio work he was accustomed to. "*I'd have to say the same line 50 or 60 times to get it in sync with the mouth of the plant.*"

"*They told me to be the voice of a plant that starts out as a pod and grows to 60 feet, and I hadn't seen the play the movie's based on! But [film producer] David Geffen [who picked out Levi for the part after seeing the Four Tops perform on Live Aid] was relatively sure I could do it.*

"*He wanted someone with an earthy, streetwise approach but who could be nice and cuddly at the same time. I grew up in the streets, so that part came easy. But the nice and cuddly part I had to learn later.*"

Audrey was not something of a one-off, as Levi was also to be the voice behind the evil 'Mother Brain', on Nintendo's television cartoon 'Captain N: The Game Master, which appeared between 1989 and 1991.

But back to The Four Tops. In the 'Rhythm and the Blues' column of 'Billboard' for March 21st 1987, the 'Short Stuff' snippets at the end contained the following: "*The Four Tops have left Motown again to sign with Arista, though the Clive Davis' label has yet to confirm the signing officially. Word is that the Arista executive feels he can bring back the Tops in a big way.*"

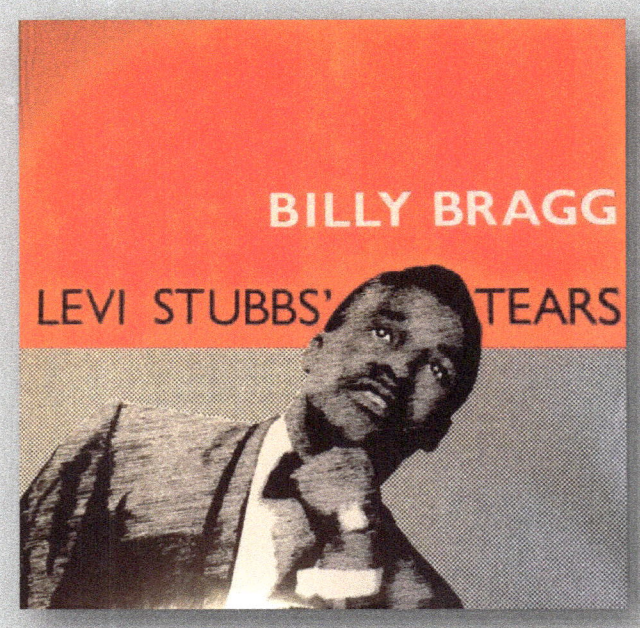

THE BEGINNING OF THE END

Having digressed slightly from the recording career of the group, we again have to back-track to that 'Hot Nights' album, often listed in discographies as 'Motown 6211' which consisted of a track listing that read as follows: Side One - 1 – 'Hot Nights'; 2 – 'Red Hot Love'; 3 – 'I Believe In You and Me'; 4 – 'Let's Jam'; 5 – 'We Got Bus'ness'. Side Two – 1 – 'This Is Love'; 2 – 'So Up For You'; 3 – 'Livin' It Up Too Much'; 4 – 'The Four Of Us' and although it was never to be released by Motown, like the proposed 'Indestructible' album, the tracks 'Let's Jam' and 'The Four Of Us' would, however, soon make an appearance on disc.

It is arguable that the non-appearance of that album circled around the group leaving Motown for the second time. "*These days music is much more of a business. That's why when we rejoined Motown a few years ago for its 25th Anniversary it didn't work out*", commented Obie. "*The whole company had just got too big. It was no longer the family organisation that we remembered it as. There was no warmth, so we had to leave, this time for good.*"

For many, who had been around for so long, they would have simply shrugged their shoulders, been content with the longevity that they had enjoyed, both on the road and in the studio, and called it a day. But Levi, Duke, Lawrence and Obie still found enjoyment in what they did and although the chorography might be a little subdued from what it was, they could still hold an audience on the palm of their hands.

This ability to out-perform others, despite their failure when it came to chart success did not deter the Arista label from adding them to the books, heralding a new era for the group that had been together for an astonishing thirty-four years.

It is arguable that The Four Tops arrival at Arista could have materialised through their friendship with Aretha Franklin, who was well connected within the label since the start of the eighties following her departure from Atlantic. In any case, the meeting of the two giants was to see them once again in the studio together, recording '**If Ever A Love There Was**', released in 1988, which would be featured on the soundtrack of the film 'I'm Gonna Get You Sucka'.

Upon leaving Motown, the foursome took with them, reported in some quarters as having to buy them back, pre-recorded tapes of tracks that were ear-marked for that binned 'Hot Nights' album and the proposed 'Indestructible' one.

Settling in at Arista, they were soon in the studio recording their album 'Indestructible', the title no doubt annoying the powers at be at Motown, but who cared? From the album came the single of the same name, coupled with 'Are You With Me'. The impression the 7" release made on the American charts was relatively minor to say the least, R&B No.57 and pop No.35.

The success of that single in the U.K. was more favourable, hitting the No.30 spot, a major triumph considering what could be seen as their recent failures.

Such placings could be considered strange, as reviews of the album had been favourable. 'Cashbox' had commented: "*The Four Tops will release Indestructible, their debut LP for Arista Records on September 1. The Tops departure from Motown Records marks the beginning of a new era in sound and style for the group. Indestructible will offer new directions for the Tops with collaborations by Phil Collins, Aretha Franklin, Huey Lewis and superstar producer Narada. Cuts form the album include "If Ever A Love There Was," "Going Loco In Acapulco" and "Are You With Me."*".

'Billboard' was to ask the question: "*What do the Four Tops need to get back to the top?*"

"The only reason they haven't sold big in recent years is the reason most acts don't sell: They didn't have hits," says Jim Cawley, Arista VP of sales and distribution. "Most groups need hits to sustain sales. As soon as [the Tops] have them again, they will sell a lot of albums again."

The Tops' debut Arista album, the new "Indestructible," is the vehicle the long-lived quartet hopes will take it skyward again. The album boasts contributions from Smokey Robinson, Clarence Clemons, Kenny G, Aretha Franklin, Phil Collins, Lamont Dozier, Huey Lewis & the News, and Narada Michael Walden. The album's title track, which recently entered the Hot 100 Singles chart, is featured on Arista's "Summer Olympics" album and will garner additional airplay during NBC-TV's coverage of the Games. "Yuppies" is how Cawley characterizes the veteran band's target audience. "I hate to use that word," adds the label exec, "but we're looking at 35-year-old men and women who work at ad agencies, the stock market, or whatever. When they leave work, they're going to be listening to the Four Tops on the way home or chill out with it at night. We're going to be tapping into the millions of people who bought [Four Tops] albums."

In the U.K., however, 'Record Mirror' reviewer Johnny Dee was considerably negative, not to say scathing, in his review, writing: "*In a way the Four Tops only made a "comeback" in the public eye because a group of impersonators were making a lot of money using their name in Med holiday resorts. Their return is also quite a sign of the times - golden oldies seemingly being more popular than current chart hits on national radio.*

"*So, if other people are making a handsome profit by rehashing past legends it only seems fair that the legends themselves should make a buck too. Reasonable, but ultimately very sad indeed.*

"*This LP makes a mockery of their Motown back catalogue, totally lacking emotion, soul and melody. One can only conclude that the impersonators had more of an idea what the Four Tops were about than the real Four Tops - the tourists,* although miffed at being ripped off, all admitted what a good show they put on! Imagine how embarrassed Billy Bragg must have felt when he first heard 'Loco In Acapulco', after writing 'Levi Stubbs' Tears' - a song about the Tops singer's soul! Personally, I can't wait for Russ Abbott to do a cover version of 'Loco' - which he surely will - on one of his fun party records. Then justice truly will be done! The problem with legends is they don't know when to call it a day."

Dee was forced to eat his words, as '**Loco In Acapulco**' b/w '**Change Of Heart**' not only filled countless dance floors across the country, but gave The Four Tops a top ten U.K. hit, peaking at No.7, perhaps with some publicity from the film 'Buster' starring Phil Collins in which it featured.

Written and produced by Lamont Dozier and Collins, the former Motown man, was to immediately think of his old studio friends and told his co-writer that the track was ideal for the Tops. A telephone call was made and a day later they were in the studio laying down the vocals.

It is interesting to note that in America, 'Loco' was relegated to the 'B' side, with 'Change Of Heart' pushed as the top side, so perhaps it was not surprising that it made little impression on the general public.

Further embarrassment would have been heaped on Johnny Dee, coming from a later 'Record Mirror' article which contained the following: *"The Four Tops are a phenomenon. Just as it looked as though they would be consigned to endless revues at Las Vegas alongside Franki Valli and The Four Seasons, they strike gold with 'Loco In Acapulco' and again with 'Indestructible', and they're back on the road, enjoying the same attention as they did 25 years ago at the height of Motown's success."*

Speaking following a concert at the Brighton Dome where the guys, having received a rapturous reception from the full-house made up of teenagers, adults and pensioners before drifting through medleys of their hits in something of a sing-along, as everyone knew the words, Obie was to say: *"Of course it's great to have hits again, it's like having a second chance. But I mean, we have twenty-five grandchildren between us now, and yet it's still young people buying our records. It makes us feel that we can still communicate across age differences. That's special."*

When asked if it was any different from their sixties heyday Lawrence replied: *"Not a whole lot. Obviously, we're not so wild now. In those days we'd come offstage and party all night. We couldn't do that now, we just don't have the energy! When we're in Vegas amongst all the gamblers and high rollers we hang out a little more, but only because you never know what time it is - in all these halls and casinos they don't have clocks and unless you go outside you've no idea whether it's night or day!"*

"I think the whole scene is less exciting today," continued Obie. *"Maybe I'm just being nostalgic, but back in the Sixties, when we were with Motown, life just seemed to be so exciting, so much atmosphere. These days music is much more of a business. That's why when we rejoined Motown a few years ago for its 25th Anniversary it didn't work out. The whole company had just got too big. It was no longer the family organisation that we remembered it as. There was no warmth, so we had to leave, this time for good."*

But how long could they keep on performing? *"We'll let the audiences decide that,"* says Obie. *"It's one of those businesses where you can keep on going for as long as you want to. There are groups much older than us - look at the Mills Brothers, some of those guys are in their eighties. As long as we're happy doing it and people are happy seeing us we'll carry on."*

That decision as to how long the group could go on had almost been taken out of their hands in December 1988.

In London to record a segment for Top Of The Pops, the show's producer wanted two performances recorded, which the group were happy to do, but the former wanted to schedule them over two days, while the Tops wanted to do them back to back as they wanted to get back home for Christmas and had seats booked on what was to be the ill-fated Pan Am Flight 103.

Arguments ensued, but it was the producer who got the final say and a night in a hotel had to be booked rather than a taxi to the airport.

Having just flown over the Solway Firth and the coast-line of south-west Scotland, the plane exploded as it neared Lockerbie [the flight path clearly visible from this writer's back garden], immediately killing all 259 people on board and 11 more in the small Scottish town.

The group, however, had no idea of the tragedy that had unfolded until Levi telephoned his wife to tell her that he and the others had missed the flight due to the Top of The Pops filming. Stunned by her outbreak of emotion amid sobs and tears, she explained what had happened a few hundred miles away.

Avoiding death, back in the charts, life was certainly good.

A review of a concert at Manchester's Apollo, by David Giles, which appeared in the good old 'Record Mirror' in February 1989 read: *"The chap just in front of us is positively beside himself. The one bright spark in an initially sedentary audience, every now and again a note, a harmony, an announcement, brings him rearing to his full height, punching the air and hollering. As in 'Levi Stubbs' Tears', this is how to heal those emotional wounds. That's why it's called soul music.*

"It's been over five years now since the Tops last graced these stages, and time is beginning to take its toll. As Levi and the fellas sweep across the stage, decked out as ever in immaculate, pristine white suits, you can tell that they're getting a bit - how can I put it - portly. Not quite as trim as of old.

"They still sing like canaries, of course, though these days they have to take it easy. Like, closing down the show after less than an hour (the house lights were on even before the orchestra had had a chance to leave the stage!).

"Like, not getting out of bed before five o'clock. But that's Motown legends for you.

"Very little of the 'Indestructible' LP is aired, which is just as well bearing in mind the show's brevity. Instead, they play quite a few forgotten nuggets, like 'Main Street

People' and some of their not-so-distant hits like 'When She Was My Girl'. The old-style orchestra (mostly brass) helps to fabricate the illusion of Sixties America.

"Real showbiz stuff. And the old magic's there in between the wrinkles. They launch into an extended medley of classics, the four voices swooping on the listeners, cradling and comforting us. By now the bloke in front has vanished. He's gone. Up there with the stars, in the Milky Way."

Patience, they say is a virtue and that all good things come to those who wait. Some, however, have to wait longer than others to receive what they deserve, which was certainly true in the case of The Four Tops.

Less than a handful of years short of four decades in the music business was to see them finally receive the recognition they deserved, out with record sales and standing ovations, when it was announced in November 1989 that they were to be inducted into 'The Rock and Roll Hall Of Fame'.

With an unchanged line-up throughout that whole period, it was never a case of look over your shoulder, as no-one came close to them as a vocal group.

After receiving the award, Duke commented: "*That was amazing. That was the epitome of what you do. To be inducted into the Hall Of Fame for what you do, that's the epitome. You don't ask for too much more than that. You've done enough for your peers to elect you on the first ballot and say that you're one of the best to do what you're doing. It was absolutely amazing. It was probably one of the greatest things that we had accomplished.*"

Life at Arista would be short lived, but nevertheless, that brief stay worked in the groups favour, projecting them once again into the eyes of the current media and they were to see out their contract at the

label with 1989 producing the aforementioned release of 'Change of Heart', while Europe was to be afforded **'The Sun Ain't Gonna Shine (The Ben Liebrand Remix) – an essential dance mix and a single version'** b/w **'A drum Cappella Mix and a PH Balance Mix of Loco In Acapulco'**.

1989 was to see them back on British shores, selling out their concert dates up and down the country, with the national and local press keen to fill half a page or a mere couple of paragraphs on the ever-green group.

One concert, at the familiar Hammersmith Odeon, saw 'Daily Express' writer Paul Simper write: "*HIT Man Pete Watermap has found a fond idea that his bristling young stable of Ricks, Kylies, Mandys and Sinittas is The Sound of Young Britain.*

"*Now there's nothing wrong with being optimistic, but if any of his young charges wandered into the Hammersmith Odeon the other night they would have been made to feel very small. Spanning 25 years of hit-making, The Four Tops have a track record Mr Waterman would kill for.*

"*No matter they're now four full-figured gents who tend to execute their dance routines in their own sweet time. All it takes is the cavalry charge of 'Reach Out I'll Be There' and the audience is deliriously transported.*

"*There are some big kids on-stage as well, Phil Collins, some sort of national hero judging by the roar his entrance provokes. bounds on at the outset to give it a go on 'Loco'.*

"*And Ruby Turner is all big grins and whoos as she bravely takes Aretha Franklin's place for the duet with Levi "If Evera Love There Was." But in the end the night belongs to The Tops*."

The recording studio was now to become a place of memories, strenuous sessions, pushed to the limits by Lamont Dozier and the Holland brothers, but also full of joviality and brotherhood. Concerts was now the bread and butter, 75%

of which were performed alongside The Temptations.

There would also be television work, both in America and Britain, with the former producing something of surprise appearances in 1987 and 1989 in Season 18 of the children's television show Sesame Street singing 'Please Be Careful' [episode 2256] and 'Standing At The Bus Stop Sign' [episode 2290].

Never out of favour, or allowed to be forgotten, those hits of yesteryear were frequently repacked, on countless different labels, more so with the appearance and popularity of CD's. 'B' sides suddenly became 'A' sides, but it would be 1995 before something relatively new would appear in the record stores and even then, it would have only limited appeal. Lawrence Payton would joke – "*Every time we went to England, about once a year, they would put out a new greatest hit. On some of the greatest hits, they would put on B-sides.*"

There had been a telephone call to a London hotel one morning at 4.00am, when Lawrence Payton was awakened from a deep sleep to hear the voice of Berry Gordy saying that he wanted them back at Motown.

It wasn't an offer of yet another contract, which in any case would more than likely have been turned down and the telephone immediately silenced, but a request to record the

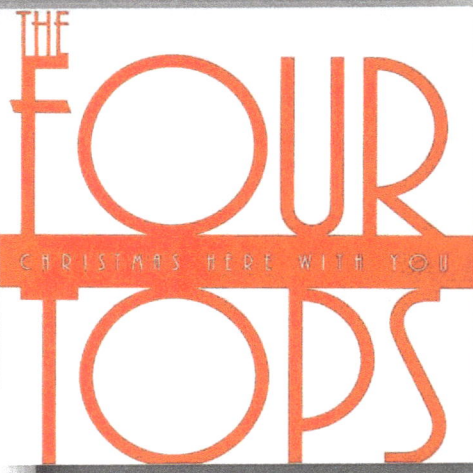

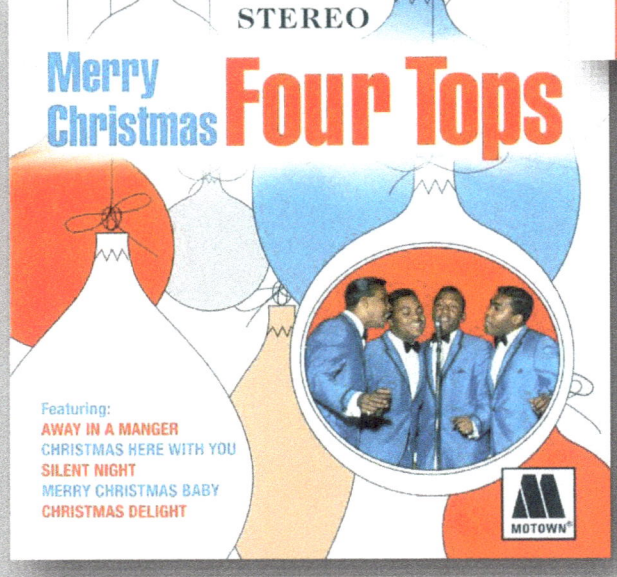

Jackson Five hit 'I'll Be There' for a planned Gordy tribute album. "*I want you to do it the way you did a long time ago when I first met you.*"

"*We did a number on this sucker and we killed. We haven't sounded like that in so long,*" said Payton. "*I thought maybe we had forgot, but all the guys came through like champs.*"

1995 would also see the release of '**Merry Christmas - Four Tops**' or '**Christmas Here With You**' as it was called in the States.

The album would see 'White Christmas' and 'Silent Night' feature Aretha Franklin, with Obie Benson and Ronnie McNeir co-writing 'Merry Christmas To You' and 'Christmas Delight' with Lawrence Payton co-writing 'Christmas Here With You'.

While Christmas was a time for celebration, the 1990's were to bring tears and the first sad step in the breakdown of the group with the passing of Lawrence Payton at his home in Southfield, Michigan, surrounded with his wife and family, on 20th June 1997 as a result of liver cancer.

He had been too ill to attend the unveiling of a star in honour of the group on the Hollywood Walk of Fame a couple of months earlier. *"These are four of the greatest people I known"* said Berry Gordy at the time. *"They were major pros, even before they came to Motown."*

Of his fellow Top, Obie Benson was to say: *"When we lost Lawrence, it was like losing part of your body."*

Lawrence was only fifty-nine when he died, still a young man and if Levi Stubbs had got his way, it would have been his voice that took the lead on 'I Can't Help Myself'.

"No way man" was the Payton reply.

It was after leaving Motown in 1972 that Lawrence came more to the fore, with his creative ability being allowed to flourish, becoming more involved in production and song-writing. Something that he

LAWRENCE PAYTON
1938 - 1997

was denied under the Berry Gordy regime.

Having knocked back the idea of taking the lead on 'I Can't Help Myself', his voice can be found out front on his solo effort 'One Woman Man', while he co-produced 'Night Lights Harmony' in 1975 and two later albums, 'Catfish' and 'The Show Must Go On'. He often shared writing credits with the Tops' longtime associate, Fred Bridges, and on 1982's 'One More Mountain' album, he co-wrote 'Nobody's Gonna Love You Like I Do' with Levi Stubbs.

The death of Lawrence Payton was a crushing blow to the others and, not for the first time in their careers, they found themselves with some serious thinking to do and decisions to make. In the past, everything had drifted along relatively smoothly, but they suddenly found themselves at a crossroads.

Initially, Levi, Duke and Obie made the decision to simply continue as a trio, but once out on the road, it simply, and obviously, didn't work. Eyes would drift across the stage to a vacant spot, haunting the others so much so that it was finally decided to seek a replacement.

Into the breach came Theo Peoples who had enjoyed a six-year stint with The Temptations, and although being hand-picked by the other members of the group, it wasn't straight forward according to 'Fox 2 now' who published the following in an article that appeared a number of years later – *"According to Peoples his new lifestyle was decadent, filled with every possible vice. Vices that eventually led to his dismissal from the Temptations after a cocaine binge caused him to miss a curtain call.*

"A dream that became more lucrative when the Four Tops came to Peoples with an offer to join

them, but there was a catch, Theo had six months to get his life together, which he did."

Theo Peoples integrated himself with the group and having watched them at close quarters whilst with the Temptations, he was more than aware of the standards that had to be maintained, but he was to find the bar raised even higher when Levi Stubbs suffered a stroke in 2000 and he was asked to move from the side to the centre.

Perhaps somewhat reluctant at first, he made the move and was soon earning the accolades from the Four Tops fan-base. No-one could have been expected to reach the heights of Levi Stubbs, still considered one of the greatest voices in soul music, but Peoples was to create his own niche.

With Levi stepping down and Peoples stepping into the breach, there was a position up for grabs. Looking for that replacement, Duke and Obie didn't have to look very far, deciding that someone with Motown etched in their CV would be more than ideal. Step forward Ronnie McNeir.

Born in Alabama, Ronnie was to see releases on the Prodigal label in the early seventies before 'Selling My Heart To The Junkman' was released on Motown, a track taken from his 1976 album 'Love's Comin' Down'. He was perhaps better known for his 1966 De-To release 'Sitting In My Class', a favourite on the Northern Soul scene.

Perhaps he didn't make much money on that recording at the time, but in later years it was to prove a nice little earner, more so when he toured the U.K. with the Four Tops, as on nights off, he would take on personal appearances at venues singing that particular track, plus a couple of the Tops recordings [his take on 'Ask The Lonely' was excellent] along with a more recent Ian Levine written and produced one.

Speaking about Levi, Ronnie was to say: "*I met him, when I met Obie. Obie introduced me to the group.*

He's one of the greatest vocalists that you could ever know. You can pick singers that sound like David Ruffin or Eddie Kendricks, but Levi had a voice hard to match. As a matter of fact, the only guy ever with a sound kind of like him was General Johnson of the Chairmen of the Board."

The show carried on, but the tears continued to flow in 2004 during the groups 50th Anniversary concert at Detroit's Opera House, when Aretha Franklin introduced the group, not the Four Tops, but the Five Tops, as joining Duke, Obie, Theo and Ronnie on stage was the wheelchair bound Levi.

If the sight of the once energetic lead singer being wheeled on stage was not enough to tug at the heart strings, those tears flowed freely as the song 'I Believe In You And Me'

- 100 -

echoed around the auditorium via Theo and Aretha.

Prompted by Obie, an often-tearful Levi struggled through the song as best he could, as emotions ran high both on stage and in the audience. It was a performance to remember. More so as it was his last time on stage with his fellow Tops.

2005 was to see the group once again thrown into disarray, as a circulation problem was to see Obie requiring surgery to amputate a leg, which in turn saw him suffer a heart attack. Subsequently, he was diagnosed with lung cancer and had begun intense, stage four chemotherapy treatment only a week prior to his untimely death on July 1st at Harper University Hospital in Detroit.

He had made what was to be his farewell appearance on the Late Show With David Letterman on April 8th of that year.

Known as the joker within the group, Duke Fakir was to say: "*He enjoyed every moment of his life. He put a smile on everyone's face, including my own.*"

He was also responsible for much of the groups concert choreography and is perhaps remembered just as much for his collaboration in Marvin Gaye's 'What's Going On' than his time with The Four Tops.

RENALDO 'OBIE' BENSON
1937 - 2005

Following Obie's passing, the continuation of The Four Tops resumed by keeping it in the family, as his place was taken by Lawrence [Roquel] Payton Jr., but within three years, that line-up had changed again.

The announcement on October 17th 2008, telling the world that Levi had passed away, although not coming as a great shock due to his on-going illness, was still filled with sadness.

Over the years, there has been numerous great 'soul' singers in the likes of Jackie Wilson and Marvin Gaye to name but two, but in the opinion of many, no-one could touch those spine-tingling, baritone vocals of the Four Tops front man.

Levi would deny that he was the 'front man' as he always considered himself nothing more than a member of the group. So much so that he turned down a part of Louis McKay in the Diana Ross as Billie Holiday film 'Lady Sings The Blues' as he was not a solo artist, but a member of a group and didn't want to project himself out in front of the others.

"*He could do anything with his voice*" said Duke Fakir in the aftermath of his passing. "*He could take you anywhere with it. He could take you to a love scene. He could take you dancing. He could take a great old standard and make you feel like you're right there in that song.*"

It is arguable that he didn't realise his vocal capabilities, as one recording session, under the watchful eyes of the Holland-Dozier-Holland trio was to see him fail to deliver what was required. Knowing that there were a handful of fans sitting on the steps outside the Hitsville studio, and knowing how much Levi enjoyed performing in front of an audience, they were invited inside. Installed in the studio, the tape was once again allowed to run and this time Levi nailed it thanks to his 'audience'.

Whether it was the piercing cry of 'Bernadette' or the pleading vocals of 'Ask The Lonely', his was a voice that instantly hit the spot, leaving you in no doubt that you were listening to something special.

The tributes were many, and justifiably so. Otis Williams of The Temptations, who had shared the billing with the Tops on countless occasions was to recall a visit by the wheelchair bound Levi prior to a concert: *"We had him in the dressing room and sang 'Baby I Need Your Loving' ... He would try to sing along with us, and as he was singing you could see tears well up in his eyes. He just longed to be on stage and do what he was known to do."*

Williams was also to call Levi *"our black Frank Sinatra. Frank not only had the voice but what made Sinatra unique was the way he'd phrase the song. Levi had that same kind of talent; whatever he was singing he would phrase it so uniquely that you would just stand there in awe."*

"The greatest interpreter of songs I've ever heard" echoed Berry Gordy, adding, "*It is not only a tremendous personal loss for me, but for the Motown family, and people all over the world who were touched by his rare voice and remarkable spirit*", while Brian and Eddie Holland added: *"Working with Levi was one of the most inspirational aspects of the time we spent at Motown. Just listening to the way he was able to deliver the HDH songs brought more beauty to them than we could have imagined ... He was an inspiration to us as songwriters and producers."*

Unlike most singers, Levi's voice was one that could not be imitated and it was a voice that was comfortable whether singing the songs of Broadway, something that had a leaning towards jazz or those he made famous at Motown. It was a voice that was instantly recognisable.

"As each one of them passed, a little bit of me left with them." said Duke Fakir. *"When Levi left us, I found myself in a quandary as to what I was going to do from that moment on but after a while I*

LEVI STUBBS
1936 - 2008

Celebrating His Life

LEVI STUBBS, JR.

Sunrise: June 6, 1936   Sunset: October 17, 2008
Monday, October 27, 2008
Visitation 10:00 am   Service 11:00 am
Greater Grace Temple
23500 W. Seven Mile Rd., Detroit, MI
Bishop Charles H. Ellis, III, Officiating

realized that the name, together with the legacy that they had left us, simply had to carry on and judging by the audience reaction it soon became pretty evident that I did the right thing and I really do feel good about that."

There was no replacement required on this occasion and the group continued to tour with the line-up of Duke Fakir, Ronnie McNeir, Theo Peoples and Roquel Payton over the course of the next couple of years, until Theo left in 2010.

HAROLD BONHART

Left is a debatable word, as numerous sources say that he was fired, which in turn was met by disbelief in some quarters as he was considered the guy who held the group together following Levi's sudden departure.

J. ALEXANDER MORRIS

To replace Peoples, in came former Spinner's member, Detroit born Harold Bonhart, who was to remain with the group until 2018 when he in turn was replaced with J. Alexander Morris who became the groups lead singer.

Being a member of a world renown group would project you into the public eye, but when looking back at his time as a Top, the headlines swing from acclaim to despair, with Morris becoming involved in a lawsuit from events in 2023 that he could do little about.

Arriving at Ascension Macomb Oakland Hospital in Marren, Michigan in an ambulance, complaining about having difficulty in breathing and chest pains. He was noted to have a history of cardiac disease.

Upon his arrival, he was allegedly denied medical treatment due to his race and/or perceived mental disability, having informed a nurse and a security guard that he was a member of The Four Tops and had concerns in regards to stalkers and fans. This latter information was not believed and a psychological evaluation was sought, which lead to him being restrained in a strait jacket. "*It was a terrifying experience to be in the middle of a medical emergency, to be placed into restraints, to have my oxygen turned off, my personal effects taken from me, and no help from the doctors and nurses because of the colour of my skin. Racial profiling nearly cost me my life,*" Morris was to say in a statement.

Hospital staff were soon to recognise their error when he played them footage of a performance at the Grammy Awards and he was offered a $25 gift card as an apology. Morris in turn announced that he was planning to sue the hospital, which continued to be under investigation.

2018 would also see Duke in hospital, although in the fashion of a true entertainer, it was a case of 'the show must go on'.

Having previously endured a hip replacement, forcing him to miss his first ever show, he slipped in a hotel room prior to a show in Pennsylvania and fractured his other hip. Advised to cancel the show and go to hospital, he brushed away those suggestions, did the show, despite being in some pain, got on the tour bus and headed back to Detroit.

Upon arrival, his wife refused to allow him in their house, sending him immediately to see his doctor which resulted in the eventual hospital appointment.

If a fractured hip wouldn't stop Duke performing, then Covid-19 certainly did, as concerts were forcibly cancelled, giving him, and the rest of the group, a well-earned rest. They were, however, soon back on the road.

With Duke being considered the spokesman for the group, it came as little surprise that he would go into print, with "My Life With The Four Tops" published in May 2022, which was eagerly received.

But as the days, weeks and months passed, Duke found himself in a quandary. He was not getting any younger and had begun to struggle with his mobility, other ailments being also thrown into the mix. Touring was a young man's game and undoubtedly, being the last man standing had more than an on-going effect on him, as obviously had the passing of his fellow group members and close friends like Aretha Franklin and one-time live in lover Mary Wilson of The Supremes.

So, as the re-releases of those instantly recognisable songs continued to flow on a regular basis and a forthcoming tour with his one-time Motown stable mate Martha Reeves, backed by disco favourites Tavaras, looming on the horizon, the news broke that Duke

people so much enjoyment over the years through their extensive Motown catalogue, time with his family in the latter years of his life was the least the Four Tops fan-base could wish for him.

Fakir was hanging up the microphone, confining his stage outfits to the wardrobe [or perhaps the Motown Museum?] and calling it a day.

He had written in his memoir: "*I'm not going to ever retire, the Lord can retire me, but I'm not going into the dark night quietly. I know I'm not in the fourth quarter anymore. I'm in overtime.*"

If anyone deserved the life of a retiree, then it was Duke Fakir. Along with his boyhood friends, Levi, Obie and Lawrence, he had given millions of

It was therefore back to the recruitment process and stepping into the void came Michael Brock.

With a stand-out tenor voice, the native of Brenton Harbour, Michigan, he had been a member of Ali Woodson's Emperors of Soul vocal group and later became a member of The Dramatics.

Duke's retirement, however, was to be short lived as no sooner had his replacement in Michael Brock been announced than the news filtered through that Duke Fakir had died at his home in

Detroit due to heart failure at the age of eighty-eight.

A statement from the family read: *"Our hearts are heavy as we mourn the loss of a trailblazer, icon and music legend who, through his 70-year music career, touched the lives of so many as he continued to tour until the end of 2023, and officially retired this year.*

"As the last living founding member of the iconic Four Tops music group, we find solace in Duke's legacy living on through his music for generations to come."

The tributes were many and heartfelt. *"I am deeply saddened"* said Berry Gordy upon hearing the news. *"Duke was a very special member of our Motown family, and that the Tops always amazed me with their showmanship, class and artistry. He was smooth, suave and always sharp. For seventy years he kept the Four Tops' remarkable legacy intact. I so appreciate all he did for the Four Tops, for Motown and for me…Duke will be greatly missed and will always be a significant part of the Motown legacy."*

Having not only shared the Motown studio with Duke, but also enjoyed his company on the countless tours that The Four Tops and The Temptations shared billing on, Otis Williams became a close friend *"I spoke with Duke a few weeks ago to check in and see how he was doing. I saw him earlier this year and spent time with him at his house. We sat and talked in his living room and reminisced. He was so happy. We talked about Hutchins Junior High School where we met. Duke was such a sharp dresser. I'm at such a loss. He is now with Levi, Lawrence and Obie, singing for God. I miss you and love you, brother."*

"My brother, I really hate to have to say goodbye", wrote Smokey Robinson, *"but you've been called home by the Father to once again join Lawrence, Obie and Levi and make more of the heavenly music you guys made while here. I'm gonna miss you, my brother."*

For many, the death of Duke Fakir was the end of the line, the final terminal of The Four Tops journey.

The Four Tops would always be Levi Stubbs, Lawrence Payton, Obie Benson and Duke Fakir and as long as one of those four names remained within the group, they were still justifiably 'The Four Tops'.

But now, the tide had turned and those who remained, no matter how long they had been members of the quartet, were not The Four Tops. In name, they certainly were, but that was all and to many, they were now nothing more than a tribute band, going out on stage and singing all those hits of yesteryear.

ABDUL 'DUKE' FAKIR
1935 - 2024

Yes, Ronnie McNeir could do a more than capable rendering of 'Ask The Lonely', but he wasn't Levi. From the stage, the hits would continue to flow, the audience, arguably of a certain age, would sing along, word perfect, but it would have been little more than nostalgia that would have brought them to the venue, a night out. It certainly wasn't the same, never would be, nor could be. The Four Tops were no more, but their music will live forever.

PS. Check out the 2001 Hip-O Records CD 'Fourever' for the ultimate collection of Four Tops recordings.

SEARCHING FOR THE TOPS

Memorabilia, be it sport or music based, conjures up a very lucrative marketplace, with items changing hands for what can be mind boggling sums of money.

In this final section of the book, I am not going to even try to attempt to put prices alongside anything Four Tops related – there are price guides out there for records which can be consulted, but at the end of the day, an item, be it a record or whatever, is worth only as much as the next person is willing to pay for it.

Anyway, what can we dig up in

relation to The Four Tops? Concert programmes, signed photographs and goodness knows what else, but it was for their music that they were famous for, so...

Albums and singles were the staple diet of the record buying public, but there was also, another seven-inch piece of vinyl available, that in later years was to become more of a collectable item for the connoisseurs than a 'must buy' at the time of its release – the EP.

The main reason behind its failure to sell in large quantities was more or less down to the featured tracks having already appeared as single releases and on albums, hence its relatively short 'shelf life' which in turn saw it deleted much sooner than its counterparts, hence their collectability today.

Between 1961 and 1967 Motown issued twenty-five EPs in the UK, two of those by The Four Tops – **TME 2012** simply entitled 'The Four Tops' and featured 'I Can't Help Myself', 'Ask The Lonely', 'Something About You' and 'The Same Old Song' and TME 2018 'Hits', which included the next four big-sellers 'Reach Out', 'Loving You Is Sweeter Than Ever', 'Standing In The Shadows Of Love' and 'Baby I Need Your Loving'.

That meagre output, however, was surpassed across the English Channel in France, where seventy-four EP's were released over that same period of time.

There were also a further sixty-eight EPs issued via Pathe-Marconi [sixteen on Columbia and fifty-two on Tamla Motown, due to EMI's overall European distribution arrangements.

Breaking it all down to just The Four Tops, their first EP was to appear in France – **ESRF 1613** in November 1964 and entitled '**Without The One You Love**' and issued on Columbia.

As with the majority of EPs, it consisted of four tracks – 'Without The One You Love (Life Is Not Worthwhile)', 'Love Has Gone', 'Call On Me' and 'Baby I Need Your Loving'.

Of their seven French issues, this one is arguably the most difficult to find.

The other French issues were –
TMEF 511 – January 1965 - 'I Can't Help Myself', 'Sad Souvenirs', 'Ask The Lonely' and 'Where Did You Go'.
TMEF 522 – October 1965 - 'Something About You', 'Feels Like Fire', It's The Same Old Song' and 'Your Love Is Amazing'.
TMEF 535 – November 1966 - 'Reach Out I'll Be There', 'Until You Love Someone', 'Shake, Me Wake Me (When It's Over)', 'Loving You Is Sweeter Than Ever'.
TMEF 537 – January 1967 - 'Standing In The Shadows Of Love', Since You've Been Gone', 'Helpless' and 'Just As Long As You Need Me'.
TMEF 545 – May 1967 - 'Bernadette', 'Brenda', 'I Got A Feeling' and 'Then'.
TMEF 551 – June 1967 - 'Seven Rooms Of Gloom', 'Darling I Hum Our Song', 'I'll Turn to Stone' and 'Is There Anything I Can Do'. Note, There is a miss-printed issue which gives the title as 'Seven Rooms Of Bloom'!

The groups increasing popularity c.1966/1967, saw their records were available in all four corners of the world and if you want to venture even further afield in regards to EPs then there was the Brazilian Fermata EPE 549 from 1966 – 'That Motown Sound' that included 'Your Love Is Amazing' and 'It's The Same Old Song' coupled with Martha and the Vandellas 'You've Been In Love Too Long' and 'Love (Makes Me Do Foolish Things)'.

Spain wasn't to miss out, as they had Tamla Motown M-7000, a coupling of the Tops with The Temptations, the former with 'Standing In The Shadow Of Love - En La Sombra Del Amor' and 'I Can't Help Myself – No Puedo Hace Nada Por Mi'. The latter with 'I Know I'm Losing You - Se Que Te Estoy Perdiendo' and 'I Couldn't Cry If I Wanted To - No Podría Llorar Aunque Quisiera'.

To cover all the foreign issues, be they singles, EP's or LP's, it would take a publication itself to list them all, so here we will simply look at the tip of the iceberg.

If you want something really different record wise, how about the 33⅓ rpm 7" single 'No Lo Puedo Evitar' 'Sin El Unico A Uien Amas' – 'Without The One You Love' coupled with 'I Can't Help Myself'.

Whilst mentioning the latter, how about a picture sleeve Japanese release?

From Portugal, there was 'Bernadette' - Stateside PSE 507 in 1967 – 'Bernadette', 'Shake Me, Wake Me (When It's Over)', 'I Got A Feeling' and 'Loving You Is Sweeter Than Ever'. Or for that same title track, how about the picture sleeve issue from Italy with 'Bernadette' on the 'reverse side of 'Piangono Gli Uomini'?

In Germany, there was Tamla Motown TM 4002 – 'The Four Tops Live' – 'Introduction', 'It`s The Same Old Song', 'It`s Not Unusual', 'Reach Out I`ll Be There' and 'I`ll Turn To Stone'.

Westwood One LP produced for radio play. Features Sid McCoy giving a short biography of The Four Tops, interview excerpts from the band and songs."

To get some idea of the extensive world-wide output of the group, it is more than worthwhile to spend some time looking at the excellent 45cat website

As it gives you some idea as to those foreign releases, revealing the following totals from outside the United States and the U.K.– Germany – 61; Canada – 56; Netherlands – 54; Australia – 47; France – 39; New Zealand – 39; Japan – 30; Spain – 19; Ireland – 16; Argentina – 14; Italy – 12; Norway – 12; Portugal – 12; Lebanon – 10; Sweden – 9; Belgium – 8; Brazil – 8; South Africa – 6; five from each of Finland, Greece and Jamaica; four each from Denmark, Iran, Israel, Turkey and Yugoslavia; two from each of India, Peru. the Philippines, Rhodesia and Thailand; and one each from Angola, Chile, Nigeria, Poland, Singapore and one other "unknown country". Quite a list,

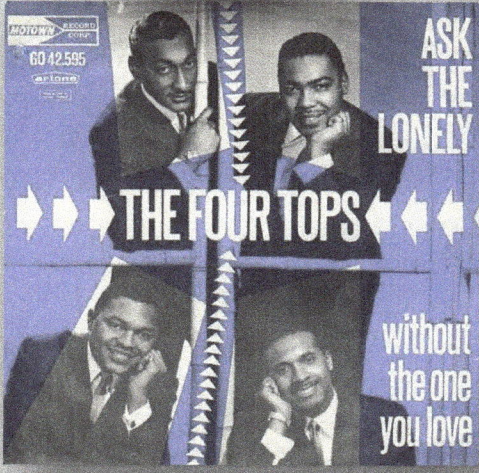

Holland was to see the excellent coupling of 'Ask The Lonely' and 'Without The One You Love', while Sweden saw the issue of an EP consisting of 'Baby I Need Your Loving', 'I Can't Help Myself', 'Reach Out' and 'Standing In The Of Love'.

Should you want something really left-field then search out Tamla Motown – TME – 7001. Issued in Argentina in 1967, it went right off the beaten track and took the quartet right back to their roots with 'Hello Broadway', 'Mame'. 'The Sound Of Music' and 'Make Someone Happy'. Just don't ask about the picture cover!

Equally left-field is the 1985 12" LP on the Westwood One label, of which little is known, other what appears on the excellent 'Discogs' website which states: *"Special*

although not all feature just the Tops, as there are odd issues that see them coupled up with another artist.

Looking through that 45cat website, one item stood out above the others and that was the solitary Polish issue – 'Reach Out I'll Be There (Wyciągnij Po Mnie Rękę)' on the Pracownia Pocztówek Dźwiękowych label.

This, going by the details on the website is a 'Postcard disc' and could actually be used as a postcard as the reverse side is laid out in that fashion.

Having mentioned that Polish cardboard disc, this was not something of a one-off, as TOPPS, who are better known for their production of trade cards of sports stars, issued a number of them in America, covering a handful of Motown acts, with two of those in the set being The Four Tops.

Issued in the late sixties and sold for fifteen cents, the disc, which

included a stick of bubble gum, was actually playable. On one side was a recording, while on the other, there was a watered-down biography of the group.

In the case of the Four Tops, there were two issues, 'I Can't Help Myself' and 'Baby I Need Your Loving'.

Before leaving the records behind, there is apparently further studio work from the quartet destined to lie gathering dust in the Motown vaults, an album that had the working title of '911 Emergency'.

Written and produced by Norman Whitfield, although Spyder Turner was quoted on the 'SoulfulDetroit' website as having written one track – 'Just Another Day (I Think Of You), those who have been privileged to hear it, or indeed parts of it, consider it to be something special.

It is disappointing that the album, has yet, to see the light of day, as not only was it marked out as an outstanding, hit strewn, concept, it was the final studio work by Levi prior to his stroke.

The track listing was as follows - 'Hoochie Mama Man', 'I Can't Help Myself' [not the oldie], 'She'll Be Back', 'Why Don't We Get Started', 'Can I Trust You With My Heart?', 'Just Another Day I Think Of You', 'Rat Race', 'Let Me Love Again', 'You Can't Run 'You Can't Run Away From Yourself and 'Emergency'. 'Emergency'.

With the mention a few lines back of the card producing TOPPS, more recent times saw the name PANNI come to the fore with their countless sticker collections, again, aimed at the sports market rather than the music one.

However, in the search for something different, up popped a few on the Tops.

From 1968, came the No.157 issue, then from 1973 came the studio shot, [top left] which was numbered 82, then a further year down the line came another studio shot numbered 93.

1974 was also to see a German issue card showing the guys in full blast.

Moving to Holland, how about The Four Tops and chocolate? From the late sixties comes 'Victoria chocolates parade of stars' No. 462, A colour photograph measuring 1¾ x 2 ½ins. While another Dutch production from Monty's Gum saw them feature in the Top Pop Set, with the card looking like a TV.

Collecting such items might not be to everyone's taste, perhaps even shunned upon by the dyed-in-the-wool record collectors, but they are all a part of The Four Tops career.

Like the records they made, it is nigh impossible to include, or attempt to discover everything there is relating to the group, but good old eBay is a huge help, conjuring up things like a playing card from Spain by FHER, dated 1968 and taken from a pack entitled 'Film and Music Stars'. Those with a red

back were issued in Spain, while a black backed set was issued in France.

Postcards are a huge collectable covering a vast number of subjects, with many carrying a very high price-tag.

1986 saw a nine-card set, issued by 'Music Nostaglia Cards' which featured music groups and included the Tops, [No.205]. The set was also to included their Motown stablemates The Temptations and the Marvelettes. On the reverse was a list of some of their hits,

Then a decade later, the same image was featured on a promotional postcard for The Complete Motown Anthology 10.

From more recent times, comes the 2005 issue from the Blue Rock Pop Music Trivia set.

Pin badges anyone? Promotional photos are numerous from across The Four Tops career, both pre and post Motown, then you have concert programmes and fliers, or how about a set of three souvenir coins from when the group were inaugurated into the Rock & Roll Hall of Fame? That is only the tip of the iceberg, as there will be so much more.

- 112 -

- 113 -

THE FOUR TOPS FAN CLUB

Fan Clubs are a thing of the distant past, a sub-culture of the fifties and sixties pop music scene when every artist appears to have devotees willing to put every waken minute and hour into an involvement with their favourite artist. The majority of which were more than happy to have someone, more than often unpaid, answer the countless letters that they had received.

In the beginning, The Four Tops did not have their own personal Fan Club, but fell under the umbrella of Dave Godin's 'Tamla Motown Appreciation Society'.

In issue No. 12 of his Society publication – 'Hitsville USA', Godin wrote that the Society would be disbanding, at the request of Motown who had suggested that instead of one organisation, there should be separate fan clubs for individual artists.

Godin put out the message asking anyone who wanted to be a secretary of a fan club for a particular artist to get in touch and he would, in due course, select the most suitable applicants.
How many applicants Dave Godin received, and for what artists, is lost in mist of time, but what is known that one of those applicants was Sharon Davis who, along with a friend, was given the go ahead to run The Four Tops Fan Club and this is her story.

If we knew what our future had in store, we would either crawl under the nearest stone or faint in disbelief. For myself, I could never have imagined in a million years that my love of Motown would lead to me joining the record company several decades later. Living in a small Sussex town (as it was then), I had dreams of somehow becoming involved in the music business but

as my first love was for black American artists, knew the chances were slight. I was a country girl for goodness sake! However, the Four Tops paved the way for me, and I never looked back. Here's a few thoughts on that journey....

I can't remember how I first became aware of Dave Godin's Tamla Motown Appreciation Society, although memories of talking to Dusty Springfield fan club members might have been a possibility as I was one of the secretaries helping Pat Rhodes to cope with her hugely successful fan club. Anyway, I joined Dave's club and delighted in the adventures of visiting artists, but, being young and miles from London, wasn't able to participate in their events.

Buying records too was quite a feat as no record shops automatically stocked Motown, so I had no choice but to have a standing order for everything released in this country. And on my secretarial salary that was a helluva stretch. Driving my parents mad with the constant Motown beat bursting forth from their hi-fi unit, I acquired a reel-to-reel machine, taped the records, and relocated to my bedroom to indulge in Motown binges that were dominated by the

Four Tops. Long story-short then, because you know how easily I get diverted.

When the TMAS closed down, Dave worked with Margaret Phelps in Motown's International Department to allocate individual artist fan clubs across the UK. I applied for the Four Tops, my first love after Martha and the Vandellas. Other clubs opened up and in time, thanks to advertising in music papers like Disc & Music Echo, all the club secretaries became friends. We were fanatical about Motown. Well, to be honest, we had to be because running a fan club, while seeming to be fun on the outside, was a costly business. Sure, Margaret Phelps provided photos, records (sometimes) and advertising material, but we needed to pay for copying the photos, the printing of membership cards and regular newsletters, and so on, as the annual membership fees scarcely scratched the surface. But we loved it!

Somewhere here you'll see a picture of one of my first newsletters, crudely printed on a stencil machine, after hours at my place of work. How I didn't get caught beats me! You should be able to make out that DJ Johnnie Walker was the clubs' president and

THE
OFFICIAL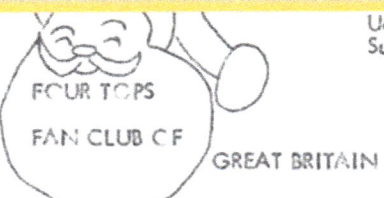
FOUR TOPS
FAN CLUB OF
GREAT BRITAIN

Uckfield,
Sussex.

PRESIDENT: JOHNNIE WALKER

HON. PRESIDENT: DUSTY

Nov/Dec. Stop Press

Dear Members,

I wanted to tell you but Motown said 'hold back - it's not confirmed'. I begged; and now the news is out, but it is not by any means definite. I know the musical papers recently have announced that the Tops are due here in January, but I heard from Motown just a couple of days ago and they still insist the arrangements are not yet settled. The foursome should arrive in Germany on the 6th January, 69, and it is thought that if the group are coming to England, they should arrive here on the 10th. Well, at the time of writing, I'm not too sure of the position but if I have any more news I'll add it at the end of this newsletter OK?

When I wrote of a "Motown Invasion" in the Sept/Oct newsletter, I didn't really expect one-so soon! Next year looks as though it could be a year to remember! But before that, things kick off with THE ISLEY BROTHERS, who are due here on the 6th December for extensive club and ballroom dates. It's also planned for the group to appear on the tele. Into 1969 now - JNR. WALKER & THE ALL STARS arrive here on the 10th January for roughly three weeks. They open at Warwick & Birmingham Universities on that date. EDWIN STARR is expected back here early next year. STEVIE WONDER opens a three-week tour on the 7th March and kicks off his tour in Big L. MARTHA REEVES & THE VANDELLAS are also due here in March. Again at the moment, I've got no details of these tours, but suggest you keep an eye - or two! - on the papers. But please don't believe all you read!

NEXT ITEM - "YESTERDAY'S DREAMS" Album. The official release date here in Britain is the FIRST JANUARY 1969! So count all your money folks cos the album is worth every penny - believe me!

"MOTOWN NOW" All the details for the next party are on the next page. You'll also find an advert. If you want any more, just send me an s.a.e. and tell me how many you need. I need not stress here, the importance of sending for your tickets almost immediately.

CHRISTMAS MAGAZINE Also in the envelope, the most eagerly awaited (I don't think!) Christmas Mag! Please don't forget to enter the competitions!? Your comments will be much appreciated! Don't be rude please!

TOPS' PRESENT As it looks as tho' the fellers may be here in January, I've decided not to send their presents to Detroit, but to wait an' give them to the group personally. So, if you still wanna send a contribution, I'll hold back buying the presents until the 16th December. Thanks to all those who've already contributed - you're very generous! Ta!

DIANA ROSS & THE SUPREMES One word - Outasight performance at the Palladium! Review of the whole affair in the next newsletter!

Now "A little bit from Sandy" - Hello there again: Just a line or two to thank you for your smashing letters about my effort of a newsletter. You're a grand lot! Maybe I can have a say again in the future but hope I'll see you at the party. Thanks again - you're great. Luv, Sandy.

NEXT NEWSLETTER : Yes, well, in the next newsletter, I'll be holding a late 'January Sale'. This'll be a chance for you all to sell your old (or new!) records. In fact anything you wanna sell, I'll advertise for you. At the moment, I'm hanging on to loads of genuine autographs from a wide selection of stars which will be selling at about a bob a time! I also have some lists of records for sale, but if any more of you wanna join in the sale, please let me know what/how/why you're wanting to get rid of by the beginning of January OK? If you want records, also let me know by then. I'll sell pictures, posters, and anything else that can be sent through the post. So over to you.....

Dusty Springfield was the honorary president. Both agreed when I asked their permission to use their names.

Other celebrities also received the newsletters. By 1970, my fan club became integrated with other clubs as Motown Ad Astra was born in London, which catered for all company acts. This decision was made with the blessing of Motown/US because several of the secretaries had relocated to London, and it was felt that dealing with one club now would offer members a better service. One thing I do remember is, we were practically crippled with import duty on records posted to us by Motown. And a social life that didn't involve the company was practically non-existent.

When acts began touring the UK in earnest, they were made aware of their fan club status and who ran them. Why this wasn't done when the club first opened, I don't know, because their personal touch in the way of a note or two for inclusion in newsletters would have been such a major coupe.

Motown visitors were young; inexperienced in travelling abroad, while bringing with them Maxine Powell's instructions on how to conduct themselves in a foreign country, reigning in any thoughts of misbehaving in public. They represented Motown and if anything distasteful was reported to Berry Gordy, they would be heavily fined and reprimanded.

Levi Stubbs, Renaldo 'Obie' Benson, Lawrence Payton and Abdul 'Duke' Fakir were, all the times I was in their company, perfect young gentlemen. Caring, engaging and oh, so suave in their persona. And, dare I risk being sexist here, so very good looking - with their boyish looks, short hair and welcoming smiles. Their absolute joy at being successful in the international world was often too much for them to accept, but their love of the UK never wavered. British fans accepted their music from the word go, and remained loyal - as only they know how to do - throughout the years that followed, irrespective of their recorded success. "British people have treated us so royally, so lovingly, over the years" said Duke one time. "Where I come from, it feels almost like a fairy tale.... Music has taken me all over the world. But my favourite trip is always to the UK. We've made so many friends over the years."

They were a credit to Motown and themselves, and while the UK was strong in its loyalty, so were the group members to each other. Despite being the lead vocalist - the voice - Levi refused to have a separate billing when others did, like Diana Ross and the Supremes, and Smokey Robinson and the Miracles. He also turned down solo opportunities to stay with the group, his family in music. And I loved this about him and them; they looked out for each other, while their combined love was apparent when we met. I digress....

Anyway, armed with said membership card, I was able to visit my favourite group when their tours included venues near my home town. One such concert was in Brighton, and as my mum was such a huge asset to the fan club by collating and posting the newsletters, I took her to see them. The concert was fabulously exciting and extremely noisy from screaming fans, while backstage adrenalin ran high. If you think theatre backstages are rubbish these days, let me assure you, back then they were dire. Dressings rooms were uninviting places to be in, while corridors and walk ways were on the dark side. Yet it was all part of the excitement of being in a different world (no pun intended).

Once introductions were over, mum and I settled into comfortable conversation with the group, highlighted with Levi opening a bottle of champagne, and handing round glasses of fizz. They asked questions about the British music scene, and I suppose, we were curious to find out about their lives.

It would be a familiar pattern with visiting Motowners because they always wanted to know about our music, particularly The Beatles - and any chance of meeting them! Then it was time for mum and I to leave that dressing room in Brighton, as other people were chomping at the bit to get in. So, it was hugs all round, with Levi kissing my mum on the cheek. A lovely gesture we smiled as we left, yet when she told my dad afterwards, he was not happy. How dare a black man kiss his wife. Mum and I were so ashamed at his words, and sickened at such narrow-mindedness, that when we'd finished berating him, we refused to talk to him on the journey home. However, I'm happy to say, it was an isolated incident yet sadly indicative of the thinkings of some people during the sixties.

I caught the group in concert wherever I could. However, one London concert in particular I missed - but another more than made up for it.

The Four Tops took the city by storm in 1966 with a couple of sell-out concerts at the Saville Theatre on 13 November. The Beatles' manager, Brian Epstein, who owned the Saville at the time, promoted the visit following a trip to Detroit to see the group. He paid them $32,000 to appear on the Sunday before "Reach Out I'll Be There" topped the UK chart, Motown's second chart-topper after The Supremes' "Baby Love" two years earlier.

The "On Top" album was released to coincide with the two shows.

Support acts were Cliff Bennett and the Rebel Rousers, and Bob Miller's Millermen, with compere Tony Hall. While in the city, they also covered radio and television, including a spot on Ready Steady Go! "Brian set up (the concerts) and made it possible for us to be accepted in the UK" recalled Duke. "He promised something and he made it come true. I'll never forget him."

Then, when told "Reach Out I'll Be There" had hit the top spot, Lawrence gushed over the Atlantic phone "You British started something in the charts over here...It's a great sound and I reckon your music has become a permanent part of the American scene. So it's a great honour for us to have a big hit with you."

Duke Fakir remembered the recording session for the chart-topper because Levi was deliberately pushed to the top of his vocal range "to make sure he'd have that cry and hunger and wailing in his voice." When the track was completed, the group disliked it so much, they begged Berry Gordy to ditch it. Thankfully, the boss disagreed. Interestingly, "Reach Out I'll Be There" was one of the few songs written for them that they recorded first.

For example, Holland, Dozier, Holland penned "This Old Heart Of Mine" for them but it was given to The Isley Brothers before the Four Tops could record it. Smokey Robinson pinched "(Come 'Round Here) I'm The One You Need" to release it, albeit it in a higher key, with The Miracles. And Kim Weston released "Helpless" as a single while the Four Tops' version was relegated to an album.

The Four Tops 1967 tour, again promoted by Brian Epstein, kicked off on Saturday 28 January with two shows before fourteen thousand people at London's Royal Albert Hall, followed by sell-out performances in Liverpool, Leeds, Glasgow, Manchester, Birmingham and other major cities. Two shows were played on each date. Their support acts this time were Madeline Bell, The Merseys, and the Johnny Watson Band. Once again Tony Hall was the show's anchor. "Standing In The Shadows Of Love" was released to coincide with these nine dates. A note of interest here. For the first time in music history a special sound system was installed in the Albert Hall in an endeavour to reproduce the Motown sound on stage. We were ecstatic. My friends and I on the first row of the balcony got so carried away, we tore up newspapers into tiny pieces and threw them over the auditorium. You ask why? I have no idea. Critics too fell over themselves in praise. One glowed - "Not even in the wildest moments of our wildest dreams could any of us have imagined what happened on Saturday night at the Albert Hall. It was the Saville Theatre twenty times over. It was a spectacle on a scale you wouldn't have expected outside a mammoth film production. It was like the fanatical exultation of the Nuremberg Rallies, the incredible enthusiasm of a World Cup football crowd."

We were crying out for the Four Tops before they stepped on stage, and when they ran on the cheers soared to the roof and bounced back off the lights. I'm thinking they didn't have to work for the audience's reaction, but they did. They sang because of it and because of the love relationship they had with their audience. In the stalls they rushed forward and surged fifteen deep round the base of the stage, while behind it they stood, swayed and clapped their hands above their heads. The Albert Hall was a swaying, dancing, weeping mass of people and I was part of it. The fact that I remember the evening so vividly is testament to the grandness of the occasion. Sadly, Brian Epstein never saw the group repeat this success because he committed suicide on 27 August 1967.

While the Four Tops were making headlines and breaking records in the UK, two of their fellow groups shared the billing at Anaheim's Melody Theatre for a week with an advance pay cheque of $95,000. This was the first time Diana Ross and the Supremes and The Temptations had appeared together in Los Angeles. This successful combination led to them recording together. Another huge money spinner.

This had a knock-on effect as a certain Motown boss decided to merge the Four Tops with The Supremes (Jean Terrell, Mary Wilson and Cindy Birdsong) with hopes of repeating the 1968 success of The Temptations with Diana Ross, Mary Wilson and Cindy Birdsong. Their first album was aptly titled "The Magnificent Seven" in September 1970; UK release in May 1971, from which "River Deep Mountain High" was released. Levi and Jean exchanging lead vocals was a sheer delight. By 1971 "The Return Of The Magnificent Seven" - with the groups dressed as cowboys and indians - and "Dynamite" with its tacky front sleeve, had been released.

A melting pot of writers and producers, including Ashford & Simpson, Clay McMurray, Harvey Fuqua and Johnny Bristol, injected magic into some of the inferior material on these albums. If I had to choose, I'd say "The Magnificent Seven" was by far the superior of the three, yet perhaps that had something to do with the initial novelty element.

Returning to 1970, 23 May to be exact, the Four Tops played to a packed house at Finsbury Park, and I joined in the wonderful euphoria of their performances. Dressed in white suits, blue shirts and pink ties, they had the audience with them from the first song. I wrote, or should I say, gushed, in Motown Ad Astra's TCB magazine "As soon as the opening bars of 'Reach Out' were heard, the audience raised the roof to the point of mass hysteria. This was followed by 'Baby I Need Your Loving'. The slick choreography has gone, but who cares."

I won't bore you with the twenty-two-year-old me burning up the pages with superlatives but suffice to say, the hits were included like "I'll Turn To Stone", "It's All In The Game", and "Barbara's Boy". The venue really rocked with "I Can't Help Myself", "I Got A Feeling" and, of course, "Reach Out, I'll Be There".

A little mishap occurred at the close of their act. When the safety curtain came down, it narrowly missed hitting Obie, but cut Levi off, leaving him front stage. When He couldn't open the curtain either, he shrugged off safety restrictions to jump down into the audience, shaking hands and hugging a few, as he walked to the exit door and out into the night air!

The next night was Fairfield Halls in Croydon. Unlike the previous evening, fans rushed to the stage after the opening song, and those who couldn't get there, danced by their seats. This time, the group wore blue suits with black shirts, but their jackets were soon discarded when the temperature rose. When "Reach Out, I'll Be There" kicked off, about one hundred fans climbed onto the stage to dance and sing with them. Then when the song finished, they returned to their seats, with the group yelling "You're too much. You're beautiful, and we love y'all!" Show over, and to backstage where crowds waited for autographs. So, once they had cooled down, the Four Tops joined everyone outside to chat and sign. Hundreds of happy fans, including myself, went home that night.

That a group should bring so much joy to so many people is a rare quality. That they stayed together through the decades is testament to their love and loyalty: family is key. We lost Lawrence first. He died from liver cancer on 20 June 1997. Obie had a leg amputated in 2005 due to an ongoing circulation problem and lung cancer was also diagnosed. He died of this and other illnesses on 1 July 2005. Levi was diagnosed with cancer in 1995, and after a stroke five years later, had to give up touring. On 27 October 2008, he died in his sleep. "I lost my three best friends. We were like brothers, we loved each other, respected each other, depended on each other."

Then Duke, who had struggled with bladder cancer, suffered heart failure, and grew his angel wings to join his beloved friends on 22 July 2024.

SHARON DAVIS
[from the original published on soulmusic.com August 2024]

www.ingramcontent.com/pod-product-compliance
Lightning Source LLC
Chambersburg PA
CBHW060945170426
43197CB00025B/2998